Love's Ripening

Love's Ripening

RUMI ON THE HEART'S JOURNEY

Translated by
KABIR HELMINSKI
& AHMAD REZWANI

SHAMBHALA   *Boston & London*   2008

Shambhala Publications, Inc.
Horticultural Hall
300 Massachusetts Avenue
Boston, Massachusetts 02115
www.shambhala.com

9 8 7 6 5 4 3 2 1

FIRST EDITION
Printed in China

Designed by Lora Zorian

♾ This edition is printed on acid-free paper that meets
the American National Standards Institute Z39.48 Standard.
Distributed in the United States by Random House, Inc.,
and in Canada by Random House of Canada Ltd

LIBRARY OF CONGRESS CATALOGING-IN-PUBLICATION DATA

Jalal al-Din, Maulana, 1207–1273.
[Poems. English. Selections]
Love's ripening: Rumi on the heart's journey/translated by Kabir
Helminski and Ahmad Rezwani.—1st ed.
p.   cm.
Includes bibliographical references and index.
ISBN 978-1-59030-532-4 (hardcover: alk. paper)
1. Jalal al-Din Rumi, Maulana, 1207–1273
—Translations into English. I. Rezwani, Ahmad.
II. Helminski, Kabir, Edmund, 1947– III. Title.
PK6480.E5R49 2008
891'.5511—dc22
2007033971

Contents

Preface

IT MAY NOT BE SO EASY TO IMAGINE, but a time will come in the sincere seeker's ripening process when he or she realizes that whatever is befalling humankind in the bitter turmoil of our time is not coming a day too soon or a day too late. These moments of foreboding are driving humankind into a corner to face the evils we have collectively acquired through our age-old oblivion and long-standing exile from the Land of Eternal Peace and Love.

Despite all the misplaced values with which we are faced, it is an article of our faith that Cosmic Love Consciousness, writ large in God's abounding beauty and expressed through His oceanic compassion, is gracefully and elegantly highlighting the sacred trail toward that Eternal Abode in whatever angelic ways It deems fit.

Mysticism, and more effectively mystical poetry, is one way toward that far-reaching and desperately sought Love Consciousness, and Mawlana Jalaluddin Balkhi Rumi is categorically the most prominent among the delineators of the road map through that Sacred Homeland.

The poems of *Love's Ripening* come from two sources of his treasured corpus. One, the *Divan-e Shams*, is a sacred ecstatic love terrain barely traversed as it deserves to be, perhaps mostly because its lyrical and musical nature in the original Persian is almost impossible to render into any other language. In the *Divan*'s twenty-six hundred love *ghazal*s, (lyric poems or odes) we have the ravishing intoxication of Divine Love, and in the second source, the six books of Rumi's *Mathnawi*, (a form of metered, rhymed couplets) we have the sober aftermath, the fully matured wisdom of love.

In the faith that these selections may serve as goblets of pure wine, bringing more and more seeking souls to Rumi's Tavern of Love, and in the hope that his rising sun of love and friendship in his eight hundredth birth anniversary will ever shine on with lasting peace over all beings, I offer my humble contribution to *Love's Ripening*. I dedicate this work to all of those inspiring guides on the Path who are graced by our Beloved One to lead us out of this dark night to that ever-green Land of Eternal Peace and Pure Light.

AHMAD REZWANI, *Cotranslator*

Introduction
The Way of the Lover

Those sweet words we shared between us,
the vault of heaven has concealed in its heart.
One day, they will pour down like rain.
Our secrets will germinate in the soil of this
    universe. [1]

R UMI BELONGS to the honored category of wisdom
teachers that would include Plato, the author of
Ecclesiastes, Lao-tzu, the author of the Gospel of
Thomas, Meister Eckhart, Shakespeare, Goethe, and,
in America, Whitman and Emerson. He can stand

with any of them in terms of his intellectual contribution, and possibly beyond any of them in spiritual depth. Once, when the great German scholar Annemarie Schimmel was asked to compare Goethe and Rumi, she responded: "The great Goethe is like an immense, majestic mountain; but Rumi, ah . . . Rumi is like the sky itself."[2]

I came into relationship with Rumi and his tradition in the late seventies. From the late 1960s I had been a student of spiritual traditions, East and West, and had practiced with Zen Buddhists, Raja Yogis, and some of G. I. Gurdjieff's students. Sufism was the last of the great traditions I encountered. Having studied Latin and Sanskrit previously, I began to explore Persian through the poetry of Rumi under the guidance of a remarkable woman, Marzieh Gail, living in a small town in New Hampshire. One thing led to another, and I eventually found myself traveling to Konya, Turkey, to be with my first Sufi mentor, Suleyman Dede. I quickly recognized that while I had been acquainted firsthand with various spiritual masters—masters of will, knowledge, and consciousness—in Dede I was meeting a genuine master of Love, and in Rumi's tradition I was entering a culture of Love. It was from a man in his eighties that I experienced what it was to be loved, unsentimentally and unconditionally.

Whatever I experienced in those five years of regular visits to Konya, I can only say it felt like a process of being tuned. Dede took no credit for this great love; he always pointed to Hazrati Mevlana, which is how Rumi is referred to in the tradition. As I began to deepen in the teachings of Rumi, I found that Rumi took no credit and, instead, referred to his beloved mentor, Shams of Tabriz. Eventually, after I tracked down the hastily transcribed conversations of Shams, since he wrote nothing himself, I found the seeds of what became a beautiful garden in Rumi. I also found that Shams took no credit himself and reserved his greatest admiration for the Prophet Muhammad. Finally, looking into the life of Muhammad, I was led into the universe of the Qur'an. I refer to it as a universe because the experience of entering into its consciousness is like entering a landscape of gnosis where the Divine Intelligence directly addresses the human heart.

What the Qur'an is saying is that there is and has been only one God behind all religious traditions and revelations, even if human beings have typically distorted the simple message for their own purposes. It is all quite simple, really, and though human beings have the free will to bring upon themselves some very bad karma (read the nasty flames of Gehenna if you like, or a living hell on earth), nevertheless, the fundamental quality of the universes (note the plural) is overwhelming, breathtaking Compassion and Mercy. I was beginning to understand where Dede was coming from.

Each year my wife, Camille, and I would return as if to remind ourselves that the tangible atmosphere of love was real. And if it were real, it might be possible to somehow bring it back with us. We lived for that. And gradually, too, we assimilated some of the knowledge of love that is found in Rumi's teachings and in the primary sources of the tradition: the Qur'an and the sayings of the Prophet.

Western culture has been shaped by the concept of freedom and personal expression, particularly in America. Perhaps even our concept of love is subservient to this emphasis on individuality, so that the emphasis of the phrase "Do you *love* me?" has moved toward "Do you love *me*?" Our culture seems to be pursuing this direction unabated.

How does Rumi's teaching apply to the context of "human love" and all of its difficulties—our possessive, protective, and demanding nature? Rumi never denies the value and beauty of any form of love, but he sees every form of love as a stepping-stone to a higher love. We are always and continually searching for the one thing that will satisfy our hearts. The need for love is behind all human desires. But:

> Everything, except love of the Most
>   Beautiful, is really agony.
> It's agony to move toward death and not
>   drink the water of life.[3]

In the Sufi understanding, our unrefined substance of love is the raw material of transformation. When I was just beginning this path, I once asked a certain shaykh how he decides whether someone has what it takes to make the journey of Sufism. "I ask them what they love," he told me, "and if they love something, anything, with devotion, they have what it takes, because that love can be transformed into a higher love for Truth."

With Rumi and Sufism a new category of spiritual personality has emerged. Among the various characters on the spiritual stage—gnostics, hermits, meditators, fakirs, yogis—we can now add the Lover.

The Intellectual versus the Lover

The intellectual is always showing off;
the lover is always getting lost.
The intellectual runs away, afraid of
    drowning;
the whole business of love is to drown in
    the sea.
Intellectuals plan their repose;
lovers are ashamed to rest.
The lover is always alone,
even surrounded with people;
like water and oil, he remains apart.
The man who goes to the trouble
of giving advice to a lover
gets nothing. He's mocked by passion.
Love is like musk. It attracts attention.
Love is a tree, and lovers are its shade.[4]

Rumi's own transformation took place in the scandalous relationship with Shams of Tabriz. The scandal of the relationship was not that there was some erotic attraction (the evidence from much collateral material suggests the unlikelihood of this, and besides, Shams was an old man in his sixties) but that in an adamantly monotheistic religious context in which idolatry was the greatest sin, Shams virtually became Rumi's God.

In the Sufi universe Beauty is a significant presence, and it is Beauty, in whatever form, that awakens love. Shams's beauty must have been unearthly, transcendent, inimitable. Rumi sacrificed status, privilege, security, friendship, and family to give himself totally to this relationship.

> I am in love with You.
> What's the use of giving me advice?
> I have already drunk the poison.
> What's the use of candy?
> They say, "Bind his feet in chains,"
> But they can't bind up my crazy heart.[5]

Shams had searched the world for one human being capable of receiving his message. Rumi was, above all, that one who was capable of receiving it and passing it on to the world. They became like two divine mirrors reflecting each other, inspiring each other to new levels of beauty and realization. If the cosmic drama of Jesus is about self-sacrifice, death, and resurrection, the Passion enacted by Rumi and Shams models the revelation of Divinity in a relationship that deepens beyond the individualities of those in the relationship.

> I could reach great heights with Your love,
> and with longing for You
> I will increase a hundredfold.
> They ask, "Why are you circling him?"
> O ignorance, I am circling myself.[6]

Rumi knew deep in his heart that the love he was experiencing was leading him back to the deepest level of himself and his own intimate connection with the Divine. In the less mature stages of love we desire and want to possess the object of our love. Rumi and Shams gave themselves unequivocally to a spiritual relationship—not a relationship in which one ego would feed and flatter another ego with unlimited attention and devotion, but a relationship that would tear each down to his essence. Shams demanded of Rumi that he die in a thousand ways, for Shams knew that the secret of love is in this dying.

You have suffered much agony, but you are
    still behind a veil,
because dying was the one thing needed,
    and you haven't fulfilled it.
Your agony will not end until you die:
you cannot reach the roof without
    ascending the ladder.
When two rungs out of a hundred are missing,
the climber will be prevented from
    reaching the roof.
When the rope lacks one foot out of a
    hundred,
how should the bucket reach the water in
    the well?
O Prince, you will not experience the
    wreck of this ship
until you put into it the last kilo that will
    sink it.
 Let your candle be extinguished in the
    dawn!
Know that as long as our little stars are
    visible,
the Sun of the world has not appeared.
Wield the mace against yourself: shatter
    egoism to pieces.[7]

This kind of love is a fire that consumes everything but itself. The encounter of Rumi and Shams is something rare in human spiritual history. In the cosmic drama lived by these two great loving souls, these two greatest friends, there was no other conclusion than that Rumi would have to lose that friendship that had become the reason for his existence. And one day Shams disappeared, leaving only a few drops of blood on the threshold, probably murdered by some self-righteous thugs who thought they were doing God a favor. In a way, they were. The Qur'an says: "There is no power except through God the Exalted" (18:39).

With Shams gone, the final veil was removed, and the sun (*Shams* literally means "sun" in Arabic) of Rumi's own heart could be revealed. The love that had been awakened could now be realized as an attribute of Rumi's own self. Rumi would later be able to teach with conviction:

> There is no love greater than love with no
> object.
> For then you, yourself, have become love
> itself.[8]

The result was that Rumi was left with a profound, continuing awareness of the awesome Love at the heart of existence. He had experienced that Love with Shams, but he could not realize it for what it was until Shams was gone.

Despite his great loss, Rumi was intoxicated with the realization that Love was everywhere and in everything working its own purpose. But if Rumi had only been a drunkard of Love, we wouldn't have the great teaching he left. In Sufism it is taught that there is a sobriety that contains drunkenness. Rumi also had this sober intelligence capable of formulating a wisdom teaching that would become a guide for the soul's journey. His *Mathnawi*, six volumes of interwoven stories, poems, metaphysical discourses, and ecstatic prayers, contains enough wisdom for a lifetime. And yet the point of every story and poem, the essence of every page, is a reality not necessarily evident to the senses and intellect alone but apparent to the Heart: that all of existence is the creation of Love for the purpose of that Love to reveal itself in the full magnitude of its Beauty and Generosity.

We sense some element of the Divine in the dramas of human love. Passionate love is as close as some get to the intoxicating spiritual Love that Rumi attempts to express. Sometimes we may even confuse the two, but it would be a big mistake to think that Rumi did.

To be fair, Rumi says that no matter what attracts us, *the Attractor is One*. Behind every attraction is a longing that will only be satisfied by the Spiritual Reality that is the cause behind creation itself. Rumi doesn't dismiss any kind of love; every form of love is a stepping-stone to a higher love, but only to the extent that we develop discernment.

Even when we attain something that attracted us, we say, "I didn't think it would be like this. I thought it was something more." These disappointments either cause us to seek more blindly and desperately or help us to develop discernment. The love-addicted tragic romantic gets caught in the repetitive search for self-validation. Having had the intoxicating experience of compelling another's attention, of "being in love," the tragic romantic searches compulsively to recapture that experience. Shams of Tabriz once said,

> All of your stress and all of your troubles
> are due to your reading your own letter all
>   the time
> and not listening to the melody of the
>   Darling.[9]

Eventually we must tire of trying to possess the

various objects of love and seek Love itself. There is really no way to do this except by encountering that Love in "the root of the root of the self." Again, Shams says:

> When the compulsive, tyrannical self
> sees the inside beauty, it melts.[10]

It is then that we may realize that Love has been seeking us all along. Now, this is the awesome fact: we are profoundly loved by the Divine, and when a human being comes to know the dimensions of that love, the change it brings about is inestimable. I believe this is what happened to Rumi in his relationship with Shams. He came face-to-face with that Divine Love in a friendship of such intensity that it could have been intended by the Divine as a gift to all humanity.

> Listen, O drop, give yourself up without
>   regret,
> and in exchange gain the Ocean.
> Listen, O drop, bestow upon yourself this
>   honor,
> and in the arms of the Sea be secure.
> Who indeed should be so fortunate?

An Ocean wooing a drop!
In God's name, in God's name, sell and buy
   at once!
Give a drop, and take this Sea full of
   pearls.[11]

Now the lover realizes that to be in relationship to the Beloved a certain work needs to be done: the purification of the self, lessening the hold of the ego over us. Shams says:

This is the work of the heart, not the work
   of the mind.
The mind constricts; love unbinds.
The mind says, "Don't let go or overflow."
Love says, "Be free without formality."[12]

Of course, the human being that seeks this relationship with the Divine Beloved does not necessarily forfeit human relationship. As a matter of fact, the self-purification and spiritual discernment that the spiritual lover seeks to develop is the best basis for human relationship as well. It is as if the volatile, unstable relationship of two egos, each concerned with its own needs and satisfactions, is not a very good basis for relationship. But when a third presence is added, the relationship is transformed by the elixir of its very presence. In addition to some fifty thousand lines of inspired poetry, Rumi gave some very succinct advice to lovers:

> In generosity and helping others, be like a
>   river.
> In compassion and grace, be like the sun.
> In concealing others' faults, be like the
>   night.
> In anger and fury, be as if you have died.
> In modesty and humility, be like the earth.
> In tolerance, be like the sea.
> Appear as you are, or be as you appear.[13]

Rumi didn't compose a self-help book for lovers. But he did reveal that Love is the only Teacher and that the lessons of Love are the most significant in our lives. He demonstrated that one could live through the greatest tragedy imaginable and still trust and be true to that Love. We are drawn to Rumi not for the sentimental consolation of his love but for its courage and fierceness.

The Pull of Love

I pulled a thorn from the fence of His
  garden,
and it has not stopped working its way into
  my heart.

One morning a little of His wine
turned my heart into a lion hunter.

It's right that this separation he helped me
  feel
lurks like a monster within my heart.

Yet heaven's wild and unbroken colt
was trained by the hand of His love.

Though reason is learned and has its
  honors,
it pawned its cap and robes for a cup of
  love.

Many hearts have sought refuge from this
  love,
but it drags and pulls them to its own
  refuge.[14]

Notes

1. Quatrain 1112, translated by Kabir Helminski and Lida Saedian.
2. Received from oral tradition; paraphrased by Kabir Helminski.
3. *Mathnawi* I, 3684–3687, in *Rumi: Daylight*, trans. Camille Helminski and Kabir Helminski (Boston: Shambhala Publications, 1999).
4. Kabir Helminski, trans., *Love Is a Stranger: Selected Lyric Poetry of Jelaluddin Rumi* (Boston: Shambhala Publications, 2000).
5. Kabir Helminski, ed., *The Pocket Rumi Reader* (Boston: Shambhala Publications, 2000), p. 9, quatrain 670.
6. Quatrain 1138, in *The Pocket Rumi Reader*, ed. Helminski.
7. *Mathnawi* VI, 753, in *Jewels of Remembrance*, trans. Camille Helminski and Kabir Helminski (Boston: Shambhala Publications, 2000).
8. Translated by Kabir Helminski.
9. From *Maqalat-i Shamsi Tabriz*, unpublished translation by Refik Algan and Kabir Helminski.
10. Ibid.
11. Helminski, *The Pocket Rumi Reader*, 170.
12. From *Maqalat Shamsi Tabrizi*, unpublished translation by Refik Algan and Kabir Helminski.
13. Received from oral tradition; paraphrased by Kabir Helminski.
14. Helminski, *Love Is a Stranger*, 37.

A Note on the Translations

So MANY ISSUES arise the moment one begins to translate: What is the purpose of the translation? Who is it for? What exactly is being translated? What do we want to faithfully reproduce? So let me try to answer some of these questions.

The selections in this book began from faithfully translated literal renderings of Rumi's poetry. The great majority of them came through my friend Ahmad Rezwani, while some of the material from the *Mathnawi* began with Reynold Nicholson's standard translation. I have also had some assistance from two other friends, Raha Azar and Saeid Rahmanapah. Some subtle and obscure issues were greatly clarified

by the scholars Dr. Muhammad Javad Mahdavi and
Muhammad Reza Mesbahi.

What I bring to this work includes a basic under-
standing of the Persian grammar; a fairly deep under-
standing of the spiritual vocabulary, acquired over
thirty years of study; a familiarity with the spiritual tra-
dition Rumi represents; and a lifelong love of poetry.
Our goal here is to offer literary translations that move
the heart and are spiritually faithful to the originals.
One liberty that we have allowed ourselves is to break
the original, somewhat long lines into shorter lines,
expressive of contemporary English free verse. If
sometimes, too, a sense of economy has led us to com-
press Rumi's language a bit, at other times we have had
to use more words than he did to express ideas that
would have been familiar in his cultural context.

When we translate into another language, we
also have to choose a tone, a quality of speech that is
in some way equivalent within our own culture to the
author's language. Inevitably, some of our own voice
slips in. In the case of Rumi, his language is sometimes
intimate and sometimes sublime, sometimes raucous
and sometimes very elegantly refined. I hope we can
begin to convey some of its power and beauty.

These are poems of spiritual states. Some of them

are conversations with the Divine Beloved that we get to overhear; some of them are directly for us. It is a Sufi teaching that one of the human being's greatest endowments is the power of the Word. It is given to us as a token of the Creative Power that has been vested in every human being. May these humble renderings awaken us to the possibilities of being human.

KABIR HELMINSKI

Love's Ripening

1

*Within This
Human Condition*

Ripened Fruit

Do you remember how you came into existence?
You may not remember
because you arrived a little drunk.
Let me give you a hint:
Let go of your mind and then be mindful.
Close your ears and listen!

It is difficult to speak to your unripeness.
You may still be in your springtime,
unaware that autumn exists.
This world is a tree to which we cling—
we, the half-ripe fruit upon it.

The immature fruit clings tightly to the branch
because, not yet ripe, it's unfit for the palace.
When fruits become ripe, sweet, and juicy,
then, biting their lips,
they loosen their hold.

When the mouth has been sweetened by felicity,
the kingdom of the world loses its appeal.
To be tightly attached to the world is immaturity.
As long as you're an embryo,
all you think about is sipping blood.

There's more to be said,
But let the Holy Spirit tell it.
You may even tell it to your own ear.
Neither I, nor some other "I," needs to tell you,
you who are also I.

Just as when you fall asleep,
you leave the presence of yourself
to enter another presence of yourself.
You hear something from yourself
and imagine that someone else

has secretly spoken to you in a dream.
But you are not a single "you,"
my friend—you are the wide sky and the deep sea.
Your awesome "You," which is nine hundredfold,
is where a hundred of your you's will drown.

Mathnawi III, 1289–1303

What Will Remain

Lovers! Wake up! When the body and soul no
   longer remain,
your heart, relieved of the body, will fly as high
   as it can.

Wash the dust from your soul and heart with
   wisdom's water;
awaken, lest your two eyes be left gazing at this dusty
   place in remorse.

Doesn't everything that exists have love as its soul?
Except for love, nothing you see will forever remain.

Your being unborn is like the East
and your appointed term is like the West,
within another sky that does not look like this sky.

The way toward Heaven is inward; lift the wings of
    love!
Once the wings of love are strong, no need for a
    ladder remains.

Do not look at the world from outside, see the world
    behind your eyes;
if you shut your two eyes to this world, this world
    may not remain.

Your heart is like the rooftop, and the senses are the
    downspout;
take your water from the roof before the gutters fall
    into ruin.

Read from the table of your own heart the whole of
    this *ghazal*.
Don't watch my tongue; lips and tongues will not
    remain.

The human body is the bow, breath and words its
    arrows;
when the arrow and quiver are gone, no use for the
    bow remains.

Divani Shamsi Tabrizi 771

Wings and Feathers

Every soul receives a Call: How long will you
    linger here?
Return to your true Home.

Since our Mount Qaf of Proximity is where you
    belong,
fly cheerfully like the legendary Anqa.*

With such shackles of clay holding you down,
painstakingly undo the shackles from your feet.

---

*A mythical bird.

Leave this strange land, travel toward Home.
We are tired of this separation, please make some
   attempt.

For some spoiled buttermilk,   .
a little water from a well, and a few sweets,
you're wearing out your life in vain!

God has given you feathers of endeavor;
as long as you have life, shouldn't you learn to fly?

From indolence the wings of hope atrophy.
When the wings and feathers are lost, what will you
   be good for?

This call of deliverance annoys you,
yet you don't mind hanging around.
Beware! How happily you are lingering deep in this
   dungeon!

Heed the call *So take admonition, O you who have
   insight!**
You are not kids, why are you biting at your sleeves?

---

*Qur'an, 59:2.

What is the admonition except for jumping over
the stream?
Come on! Jump over to the other side, like a
grown-up!

Why are you pounding the mortar of carnality?
You have no moistness, you are drifting upon the wind.

God likened this world to *dry chaff.**
Why are you gnawing at it like a beast of burden?

Come on! Here is the wine. Get out from the vat!
Now purify the body after the pancake and the
pudding.

Come on! The Witness of the Soul is seeking mirrors.
Burnish the rust off the mirrors.

I, myself, have no way or right to openly describe
these truths.
Seek them from the fountainhead, if you're really
seeking.

Divani Shamsi Tabrizi 945

---

*Qur'an, 57:20.

The True Kaaba

Circle the Kaaba of the heart*
if you possess a heart.
The heart is the true Kaaba,
the other is just a stone.

God enjoined the ritual
of circling the formal Kaaba
as a way for you to find a heart.

But if your feet walk
around the Kaaba a thousand times,
and yet you injure a heart,
do you expect to be accepted?

Give everything away, but gain a heart,
and its light will stay with you
even as far as the dark night of the grave.

Bring a thousand bags of gold coins to God,
and He will only tell you:
"Bring the heart if you come to Us.

---

*The Kaaba is the sanctuary in Mecca toward which Muslims orient their daily prayers.

"As silver and gold have no value Here,
it is the heart that We demand, if you desire Me."

In the realms of the Throne, the Tablet, and the
    Pen,*
that which seems worthless, the heart in ruins,
is the most precious thing.

Don't debase it—even though distressed,
the heart is most precious in distress.

The ruined heart attracts God's attention.
How happy is the soul that practices caring for it.

Comforting the wretched heart
in its time of need and pain
is more valuable to the Creator
than performing the outer pilgrimage.†

The ruined hearts are God's stores of treasure;
great treasures are buried in these ruins.

---

* Qur'an 7:54, 7:145, 68:1.
† "Pilgrimage": literally, Hajj and Umrah.

Tie the belt of service
and become a servant of hearts,
and the way to the Mystery may open up within you.

If you yearn for holy felicity,
shed your arrogance
and become a seeker of hearts.

When the goodwill of hearts is with you,
fountains of wisdom will begin to flow
from within your own being.

The water of life will cascade
from your speech like a river;
your Christlike breath
will become a remedy for disease.

For a single Heart all the worlds came into being;
listen to the lips that recite
the subtle point of *Except for thee
I would not have created the worlds.**

---

* Divine hadith addressing the Holy Prophet Muhammad (SAW):
"Were it not for your sake, I would not have created heavens"
(*Laulaak la maa khalaqtul aflaak*).

How else would the universe exist!
This universe of rust and dirt, of planets and stars.

Silence! A description of the heart
is impossible with words,
even if every cell of your body had a tongue.

Divani Shamsi Tabrizi 3104

The Moment You Are with Yourself

The moment that you are with yourself,
the beloved will be like a thorn to you;
and the moment that you are selfless,
what use will the beloved be to you?!

The moment that you are with yourself,
you will be a prey to a gnat;
and the moment that you are selfless,
the elephant will be the game you hunt.

The moment that you are with yourself,
you are under the clouds of sorrow;
and the moment that you are selfless,
the moon will come to your side.

The moment that you are with yourself,
your beloved will depart;
and the moment that you are selfless,
you will taste the beloved's wine.

The moment that you are with yourself,
you would feel the chill of November;
and the moment that you are selfless,
winter would blossom like spring.

All of your restlessness is due
to your seeking restfulness.
Become a tireless seeker,
so that restfulness will seek you.

All of your displeasure is due
to your seeking pleasure.
Abandon pleasures, and austerity
would become a pleasure to you.

All of your frustrations are due
to your seeking your wishes.
If you didn't, all wishes would
come to you like offerings.

Love all of the Beloved's ways,
not just Her* affection,
so that the coquettish Beloved
would come to you as a desperate lover.

Were Shamsuddin, the great king of the East,
to arrive from Tabriz,
you would be ashamed,
by God, of the moon and the stars.

Divani Shamsi Tabrizi 323

Time for the Lovers

This world offers no beauty like the Beauty inside.
O my heart! Unpack your journey's luggage here.
Are you trying to scare me with war?
Let it break out if it must!

---

* The Persian pronoun is ungendered. I use *Her* in this case, to remind us of this flexibility.

We are drunk on timeless wine,
but the learned and wise
are bound to avoid fame and infamy!

We dressed ourselves in paper clothes
on which we wrote our desperate state,
then went before the Lord of Faith,
to let Him read our yearning and need.

If you are so in love with art,
why not dip yourself like a paintbrush in the paint?
Or give up your soul to the Beloved?
Or let love untie your knot?

O soul! It's time to get drunk!
O wisdom! Be a fool!

Greece was intoxicated by His face;
Ethiopia enchanted by His hair.
Go toward Greece if you wish,
or hundreds of miles away if you will.

You are enchanted by Him
and are born out of His love.
You will never be freed from this Idol,
No matter how far you flee.

He would seek you even if you were an infidel,
And if you are a believer, He will wash you clean.
Tell the latter: Be sincere;
tell the former: Become a Nazarene.

Your eyes are fixed on His garden
and your ears are tuned to His playfulness.
Become a honeybee and collect His abundance,
or dangle yourself from His date palm.

The horizon is a bow for His arrow
and the water flows by His design.
If you are straight, you'll be an arrow;
but move sideways, and you're just a crab.

In His alluring, well-ruled kingdom,
every species is essential.
Be transformed into agate and ruby if you will,
or remain stone and clod if you must.

Whether you be a stone or an agate,
you'll tumble in the torrent of tribulation,
the torrent that ends in the sea,
so be swept into this playful, joyous love.

It is a sea like the water of Khidr;*
it won't do any harm if you drink abundantly.
Unless the seawater runs short,
you have no excuse to be distressed.

Be one of those fishes
that swim and dive within the wide sea.
If you must think of the land beyond the sea,
at least follow the river Ganges to its source.

Sometimes He will put His lips upon yours;
at other times He will seat you next to Him.
If He does one, you are His flute;
if He does the other, you are His harp.

Although there is none to be His enemy,
everywhere there are those
who need to be intoxicated by Him.
Be made a goblet for His drunks,
become a defender against His enemies.

Don't long for loneliness;
don't creep into some deserted house.

---

* Water of life (that is, the fountain from which Khidr is said to
have drunk and obtained immortality).

Come forth and be a forerunner;
it's time for the lovers to present themselves.

Only those will have no wine
who are negligent of His Vineyard;
you are His Vineyard full of grapes,
so become the wine, become intoxication itself.

Be silent like a "Mary" until you give birth
to the infant who speaks
with a breath like Jesus!
Who's forcing you to stay among braying asses?

Divani Shamsi Tabrizi 2134

Don't Talk of Love to the Body

I'm about to be set free,
all at once, from my eyes and heart;

since the Soul's Sun has come up,
I've had enough of those candles and stars.

Why continue admiring the watercolors?!
O heart, behold the Painter!

Behold the Moon and the Sun!
Why be stumbling among moon shadows?

You say you're following the scent of flowers,
but there's garlic up your nose!

How desperate you are,
seeking your daily bread from the destitute!

Look to no one but the Painter
who paints over sorrows with delights,

the One whose elixir of grace transforms
hard rock into agates and rubies.

Whether you are sober or drunk,
join His feast and be liberated,

for the days have passed
when you were wandering far from house and home.

You are not a demon of the wasteland;
why don't you then take the way to Madyan?*

---

* Madyan is a town where Moses lived for eight years preceding his
encounter with the burning bush.

For far beyond this revolving sphere
is a palace with its outer walls for you.

Was not any palace that you saw belonging to
    a King?
Is not any terrace or tower ever built by a Builder?

Thousands of flowers are laughing delightedly
down in these lowlands for a promise;

thousands of candles up in heaven
are traveling around by His command.

What a Sultan, what a magnanimous One,
who spares a life for just a prostration!

You would be better off being His captive
than enslaved by your crafty carnal self.

It is by His Omniscience that any mind
is inspired with arts and ideas;

it is by His Grace that any eye
is intoxicated and enchanting.

A donkey that feeds on a cabbage patch, undaunted,
will be thrown out of the field, thrashed, and tail-
    docked.

O Love! Don't discuss love with the body.
That charming hypocrite is not of this flock.

He would welcome you with open arms
but laugh behind your back!

Go to the graveyards and hear for yourself
the laments of the carnal self.

Divani Shamsi Tabrizi 2291

The Kurd's Lost Camel

I heard that a certain Kurd
lost his camel in a desert.
He searched everywhere for it.
But after endless searching,

failing to find his dear camel,
in sorrow by the side of the road, he fell asleep
in broad daylight, his heart,
in a hundred agonies, longing for the camel.

At last after night fell,
he awoke from his sleep, his heart still sorely troubled.
The shining ball of the moon
had rolled out onto the heavenly polo field.

And there in the moonlight suddenly he saw the camel
standing in the middle of the road;
tears of joy rolled down his cheeks like April's rain.
And turning toward the bright moon, he said:
"How may I ever describe your radiant beauty?"

Now, where is the Moon that will shine a light
on this dark stage of the human theater,
so that the human intellect
may come to find what it has lost?

The Night of Power is in your soul;
why do you not appreciate it?!
It stirs you each and every moment;
why do you not stir it too?!

It has made you mad,
taken away your peace of mind;
it has suffered much sorrow for you,
so why don't you give it a seat in your soul?!

It is water and you are the stream,
so why don't you seek that water flowing inside you?
It is musk and you are the fragrance,
so why do you not diffuse yourself?!

Divani Shamsi Tabrizi 2544

Intermixed

See how love is intermixed with the lovers.
See how the spirit and the clay are intermixed.

How often are you going to see this and that, good
   and evil?
Look at the end and see how this and that are
   intermixed.

How long will you say the "known" and the
   "unknown"?
See that both are intermixed.

How often do you say this world and the next?
See that the two are intermixed.

The heart appears like the King, and the tongue is its
   interpreter.
See how the King and the interpreter are intermixed.

Mix with each other! As it is for our sake
That this earth and sky are intermixed.

See the fire and see the water! See the wind and see
   the clay!
Enemies they are, but as friends when intermixed.

The gazelle and the lion, the ewe and the wolf, are
   four opposites,
but when they sense the Hunter near, all are
   intermixed.

What a King He is! In this garden, by His grace,
   thorns and flowers intermix.

And look at this unique cloud; by its blessing,
rainwater from many separate drainpipes flows
   intermixed.

See the unity in the creation and know that
autumn and early spring are intermixed.

Even though all of these opposites seem to clash,
like the bow and the arrow all are intermixed

Chew some sugar! Be silent and take heed!
As in the mouth, sugar and censure are intermixed.

Thus does Shams of Tabriz grow in the heart.
No one is intermixed like this.

Divani Shamsi Tabrizi 2 3 8 1

A Friend in This Quarter

O heart! Even if tribulations and misfortunes
    afflict you,
you are endowed with trust in God.

Such a Presence, and yet you are in despair?
Don't be, O heart, if you have God.

You drag your garb of thoughts here and there,
yet who do you have but Him?

All the favors that He did for you so many times,
remember them, if you are loyal.

It was the Lord who bestowed your eyes and
   the eye of the heart;
why, then, are you fixing your eyes somewhere else?

Don't waste your life as it flies by;
be a goldsmith, you have the Elixir!

Every day at dawn, there comes to you a call from
   Heaven:
"Come to Us! As you are bearing Our mark."

Before this body of yours, you were pure soul,
for how long are you keeping a distance from It?

You are a pure soul in darkened soil;
I do not say that, but would you yourself allow this
   to be so?

Know yourself apart from your garment,
since from this water and earth you have taken your
   garment.

You depart every night out of your garment,
as you have hands and feet other than this.

That's enough; I said this much just to let you know:
you have a Friend in this Quarter.

Divani Shamsi Tabrizi 3146

2

The Truth Hidden within Existence

The Egg of the Body

There's an image of God deep in your heart.
You don't need to look in some other direction.
What He can subtly bestow is limitless;
It will help you to live within the world's limits.

You will find ecstasy in the company
of pure-in-the-faith Sufis
if you just step outside
this six-doored *khaneqah*.*

---

* The Sufi lodge, which, in this case, stands for the physical world.

In your own essence you have an unseen door;
don't seek the six doors, nor the six directions:
you have the unseen door
that every night you depart through.

When you do fly,
a fine thread is fastened to your feet
to pull you back in the morning
so that you won't be gone forever.

You'll come back to the prison of the womb
so your gestation may be completed.
This world of existence resembles a womb;
haven't you wondered about all of this blood?

When the soul is fully fledged,
the eggshell of the body can get broken;
then the soul becomes the flying Ja'far,*
as much as it shines like a pure gold Ja'fari.

Divani Shamsi Tabrizi 2450

---

* Ja'far, a companion of Muhammad, who, when he was killed in
battle, received wings of the soul to fly heavenward and so is called
"Flying Ja'far"

What God Plans

We make plans, unaware of what is being planned,
and what we plan cannot withstand what God plans.

The servant deliberates, and to him it seems so clear.
Yet though he plays his tricks, he can't play God.

If a good-hearted man takes a couple of steps
    forward,
then who knows where God will take him?

Don't argue! Seek the Sovereignty of Love!
For this Sovereignty will deliver you from the Angel
    of Death.

Abandon your desire and take on the light of wisdom,
for that desire would soon lead to disappointment.

Be the King's game and don't hunt your own game,
for your game will be swept up by the falcon of
    doom.

Since you are the falcon of the King, return to His
    hand,

the hand that gives you honey, the drum that calls
   you home.

No one is more trustworthy than that King;
he will not drive you away.
Ride your donkey toward Him.

All of us are prisoners of death; be assured of that.
No mere prisoner can save you from the prison itself.

Do you know why the dog barks in this
   neighborhood of submission?
To scare away those who deserve to be scared away.

Heaven forbid that the rider who is a lover of this
   road
be disheartened by the barking of the neighborhood
   dogs.

Divani Shamsi Tabrizi 652

Sometimes This, Sometimes That

I saw a tree and a fire, and heard
a voice that said, "I am the Beloved,"
calling me from the fire. Am I Moses?

I entered the desert in tribulation
and found there manna and quails.
It has been forty years now that like Moses
I have wandered in this desert.

Do not ask about the boat and the sea.
Come, behold that for years
I have been sailing my boat in this dry land.

Come, O Soul! You are Moses and in Your hand
this body becomes a staff,
and when You throw it, I become a serpent.

You are Jesus and I am
the bird You made of clay.
As You breathe in me I come alive and fly.

I am the stone pillar of that mosque
which the Prophet leaned on for support;

now his support is elsewhere,
and I lament this separation.

O Lord of the lords and faceless Maker of faces!
What face are you ordaining for me?
I know You know, and I do not.

Sometimes I'm stone and sometimes iron;
at other times I'm all fire.
Sometimes I'm a balance without a weight;
sometimes I'm both weight and balance.

Sometimes I graze here,
and at other times they graze on me.
Sometimes I'm a wolf, and sometimes I'm a ewe,
yet at other times I am the very shepherd.

They seemed important, these signs,
but how could they ever last?
Neither this nor that will last,
and only He to whom I belong knows what I am.

Divani Shamsi Tabrizi 1414

What Substance

O my restless heart! Tell the truth!
What substance are you?
Are you fire or water?
Are you human or pure spirit?

From what direction have you come?
What food have you eaten?
What have you witnessed in annihilation?
And why are you flying toward annihilation?

Why are you uprooting me?
Why are you planning to erase me?
Why are you ambushing my intellect?
And why are you defaming yourself?

All animals and creatures
are afraid of nonexistence,
except you who are setting off
toward nonexistence.

Wayfaring with such energy,
intoxicated, completely drunk,
when do you heed any warning?
Or buy anyone's sweet talk?

From the top of this world's mountain,
you are the flood flowing down
toward the sea of nonexistence,
flowing more smoothly than my breath.

The garden and spring are bewildered,
wondering what breeze is blowing you.
The lily and the cypress are enraptured by you,
wondering what flower, what narcissus you are!

The sound of a tambourine whose jingling disks
are not accompanying its rim
would not get into our ears,
like the delirious raving of an infidel
that we take no heed of.

The Moses of your love told me,
become *Do not touch me.**
Why should I not flee from everyone?
Why should I not escape from Sameri?†

---

* Qur'an 20:97.
† Qur'an 20:85–98. (Sameri is apparently one of the Israelites
accompanying Moses, who forgot Moses's teaching about the
worship of God.)

I have fled from everyone,
though I am in the midst of the crowd,
just like a Ja'fari gold coin
in a mine deep within the earth.

If gold yells two thousand times, "I am gold!"
it won't find a buyer
as long as it does not get out of the mine.

Divani Shamsi Tabrizi 2480

There Should Be . . .

There should be a shore to our ocean,
there should be some rest on this journey.

The lion of the forest is in chains;
lions should be out there in the meadows.

Fish are throbbing on the sands;
there should be a way to the river.

The intoxicated nightingale is dead drunk;
she should be singing in a rose garden and a verdant
  meadow.

Vision is tired of this dust;
there should be new lessons for our eyes.

All of these children eating mud—
there should be a tender foster mother.

The way is lost toward the water of life;
there should be Khidr to discover a Fountain.*

The heart is in remorse for what has passed;
this new year's heart should be happy with the last
    year.

There is a scarcity of sun in this city;
we want to see the shadows cast by the Divine Sun.

The town has become packed with dung worshippers;
we long for the fragrance of the musk deer of Tartary.

Does anyone know the difference?
We need to spread some musk around.

---

* There is a myth that says Khidr and Alexander set out in search
of the water of life, but of the two, only Khidr managed to find the
Fountain and drink from it.

Too many seek for childish dominance;
there should be an unwavering Dominion.

As long as death is in ambush, day is like night;
there should be a real day to our night.

When you die, this artistry of yours will die too.
You should be ashamed of these arts of yours.

Entangled as we are in the clutching hands of this
banal world,
these clutching hands should be disentangled.

Business seekers are far too many;
there should be seekers of God the Omnipotent.

There are only a few numbered breaths left;
there should be countless breaths.

The Breath of God from Yemen*
should be blowing over the creatures.

---

* Referring to the hadith related from the Holy Prophet as saying,
"I perceive the Breath of the Merciful from Yemen." The Prophet
has sensed the presence of the Yemeni saint, Uwaysi Qarani, who
knew of the Prophet's exestence through his inner sight.

Death is tending a cauldron for us;
that stew should be palatable to us.

Since remembering death averts death,
at any moment there should be this remembrance.

Any moment hundreds of biers may pass by;
the eyes should be contrite.

The kingdoms remained and the kings are gone;
there should be an everlasting Kingdom.

Intelligence was chained and vanity unloosed,
but intelligence should have the right to choose.

Wits are like flies in that buttermilk;
we should be vigilant with our wits.

From such putrid buttermilk,
this fly should be wary.

The stomach is full of buttermilk and the ears full of
    lies;
there should be the willpower to flee.

Ears are closed, so close the lips;
there should be earrings fashioned from wisdom.

And for the metaphors of Shams of Tabriz,
there should be an interpretation beyond all concepts.

Divani Shamsi Tabrizi 3144

Music of the Hour

Angelic music is endlessly pouring down from
    heaven;
are you in a state to hear it?

Or do you bow down like a donkey and worship
    straw?
Look up just for a moment! Maybe there's a sign.

It is the End of Time, and Heaven's Cask has been
    freely opened;
the Friend has come with an army of winds to unfurl
    the Banner of Wine.

Where is someone with the Spirit of a Lion ready for
the hunt?
Where is the Knight or King to drink this wine!

Dull is the common ear that does not hear this song;
tasteless is the soul that doesn't know the pleasure of
the Truth.

Maybe, just once, cry out from the depths of your
soul!
Leap from the grave of your body!

Maybe you can untie the ropes from your foot and fly
free,
safe as Heaven against all misfortune and failure.

Raise a new head out of your old self—
one no sword can strike;
enter a garden that fall cannot plunder.

I must keep silent. *Silent*. And let Love describe itself:
a happy, life-cherishing description that will never end.

Divani Shamsi Tabrizi 2442

We Are Now One

We stood together hand in hand in primordial time;*
now at last, we are one again.

We are all of one soul struggling along one path,
and all drunk with the same wine.

From among the two worlds we chose Love alone;
except for that Love there's nothing we adore.

What bitterness did our souls suffer from separation!
At long last, we are free from separation.

A ray from the Sun came in through an opening
and raised us up in dignity, however low we were.

O Sunlight! Don't withhold Your loving radiance
  from us!
Aren't we sitting in the robes of your radiance?

---

* The Day of Alast, when all souls were asked by God, "Am I
not (*alast*) your Lord?" To which certain souls responded, "Yes,
You are."

By Your radiance we are transformed into rubies;
it is because of You that we exist.

Dancing like particles before You;
in our yearning for You, we abandon all our chains.

Divani Shamsi Tabrizi 1761

Your Image

Once Your image settled into our hearts,
we found ourselves sitting in Paradise.

All of our worries of Apocalypse and Armageddon,
each turned into the face of a houri and the charm of
    a Chinese beauty.

All that men and women fear to look at,
all that stalks them, now became close companions.

The skies became a rose garden and earth a buried
    treasure;
yet, what sort of "thing" are You that all existence
    became this way because of You?

Since we saw Him we have been prospering day after
    day;
the thistle that happened to find Him became a
    flower bed of certainty.

The unripe grapes turned ripe by the sun and became
    sugary;
likewise, dark rock turned into a gem.

Many an earth were transfigured by His charisma;
the sinister turned felicitous out of His hand of
    fortune.

The darkness of the heart became an opening of the
    heart;
the waylayer of faith is now a mentor and a leader.

The dark well of suffering that was a prison to Joseph
became a strong rope to pull himself out.

Every particle is, like the army of Allah, under Divine
    command,
to the faithful servant a guarantee and to the denier
    an ambush.

Keep silent. These words are like the Nile:
one, a Copt, will drown in this blood;
another, a blessed Israelite, will be buoyed along.

Keep silent. These words are ripened figs,
but not every bird of the air will come to discover
    them.

Divani Shamsi Tabrizi 644

Keeps on Coming

The scent of the garden keeps on coming
while the presence of the Friend is with us,
that Friend who never stops showering pearls,
while the ocean's water keeps on rising.

With just the idea of His rose garden,
this field of brambles is softer than silk.
And with a carpenter like this a ladder keeps rising
to heaven—a ladder only love can build.

Moment by moment my hungry dog
is catching the scent of bread from the spirit's kitchen.
And down the lane of the lovers
the fragrance of soulfulness keeps on coming.

Bring just one act of faithfulness and take a hundred
   thousand—
from such as this, such as that keeps on coming.
Everyone who dies before the beauty of the Beloved's
   Face
keeps entering Paradise while still alive.

The caravan of the Unseen comes before the eyes
but hides from those who cling to ugliness.
How should lovely women come to ugly men?
The nightingale always sits among roses.

The jasmine grows next to the narcissus,
the rose comes to the sweet-mouthed bud.
All of these are just symbols—I mean that
the other world keeps coming into this world.

Like cream hidden in the soul of milk,
Placelessness keeps coming into place.

Like intellect concealed in blood and skin,
the Traceless keeps entering into traces.

And beyond the intellect, a beautiful Love
keeps on coming, skirt trailing, wine glass in hand.
And from beyond Love, that indescribable One,
who can only be called "That," keeps on coming.

More than this I could in the end explain,
but jealousy keeps on hurling its lance.
So I will stop. Difficult words about Him
throw everyone into a hundred doubts.

Divani Shamsi Tabrizi 2897

A Meadow, a Tree, a Firmament, a Jewel

A meadow in which all flowers seek refuge,
one that no autumn touches, in which no rose drops
    its petals.

A tree green and graceful, in the middle of the desert,
if you sleep in its shade, you wake up drunk.

A firmament toward which all souls travel,
one where Saturn is not in strife with Venus.

A jewel from the mine of pure nonexistence,
to which the heart refers when eyes shed tears.

Divani Shamsi Tabrizi 768

3

Transformation

You, Yourself, Are the Melody

Don't turn to another beggar,
you belong exclusively to Us.
Don't sell yourself short, you are priceless.

Divide the sea with your staff,
you are the Moses of the time.
Tear the robe of the moon in half,
you are the light of Muhammad.

Sweep the beautiful wine bottles off the shelf,
you are Joseph, or Sheba, the most beautiful.
Bestow a life-giving breath,
the same as the one Christ breathed.

Charge into the battle alone,
you are the Hero of the time.
Tear open the gates of the city!*
You are Ali, the chosen one.†

Take back the Seal from the demon,
you are the Solomon of the soul.
Shatter the army of stars,
as only sunshine can do.

Walk into the fire, like Abraham, purified and
    cheerful.
Drink of the Water of Eternal Life,
like Khidr, who lives forever.‡

Walk away from the corrupt!
Be free of senseless allures!
Your origin is noble, your nature awesome.

Invulnerable in spirit, your beauty comes from
    within;

---

* Khaybar, a fortress city located near Medina, Saudi Arabia.
† "Chosen one": *murtaza;* literally, "being pleased (by God)," an epithet of Imam Ali.
‡ The Prophet, who is said to be alive and enjoying eternal life.

you belong to the Majestic, a ray from the light of
   God.

What have you seen of your own still-concealed
   beauty?
One of these days at dawn,
you will rise from within yourself like a sun.

It's a shame that you're so hidden,
like a moon under a cloud.
Clear the corporeal clouds!
Reveal the face of the moon.

No mine has such a brilliant ruby;
the world has no other soul like yours.
In this world everything diminishes,
but you are soul-enhancing soul!

You are like the sword Dhulfaqar;*
your body is a wooden sheath.
Why should you be brokenhearted
if this sheath were battered?

---

* The Prophet Muhammad's sword, handed over to Imam Ali in
the battle of Uhud.

You are like a tethered falcon,
your body just a wooden shackle.
With your own claws
undo the fetters from your feet.

How happy is the pure gold
when it enters the fire,
as it may practice its artistry
and show its real value in the fire.

Don't run away, sister, brother, from the flames.
What will happen should you be put to the test?

By God, it will not burn you;
child of ancient Abraham,
it will only brighten your golden face.

Raise your head out of the soil,
grow into a tall-standing tree.
Circle the peak of Mount Qaf,
a noble bird in the Paradise of Proximity.

Be unsheathed, like a sharpened sword.
Come out of your hidden mine,
circulate yourself like the truest coin.

If sugar could speak,
what sweet words it would utter!
Play the flute of felicity!
You, yourself, are the melody . . .

Divani Shamsi Tabrizi 2840

O Hoja

We will pull your hands forth, Hoja!*
We will cut away all of your "good and evil."

However long your night of negligence and
    drunkenness,
We will shine upon it all like the dawn.

How long will you lurk
behind the veils of vanity and competition?!
Soon it will be time
for your veil to be torn away.

---

* A conventional religious teacher.

Every fruit in the garden of the world became ripe;
wouldn't you like your sour grape,
hard as stone, to be ripened, too?

Have mercy on this soul of mine,
throbbing in this snare;
can't your ears hear the throbbing?

If the eye of your heart is in agony,
your only worry should be the pricking of that eye.

If that eye is sore, red, and watery,
then seek a remedy.

The medicine for the heart and eye
has not been and will not be
procured, O Joseph of the worthy ones,
except by gazing at Your Face.

Hoja, do you understand? Do you see?
The reward for your listening will be
in what you hear.

Divani Shamsi Tabrizi 1891

As Water Flows

I should run, run to catch up in this race;
I should become nothing, I should perish,
to reach the embrace of the Soul of the souls.

I'm overjoyed, overjoyed; I've become a flame;
I should burn down the house,
I should go out into the desert.

I should turn to dust, turn to dust, till You make me
    verdant;
I should turn to water and prostrate before the rose
    garden.

I fell out of Heaven shivering like a snowflake;
will I be safe and sound when I reach the ground?

The celestial sphere is a place of nobility,
the earth a place of fatality;
I'll be free from both of these perils when I reach the
    Presence.

This earth and atmosphere
are the essence of denial and emptiness.

I have come into the heart of heresy to achieve
  faithfulness.

The Grace of the Cosmos favors a balanced love;
may my face turn to gold coin to be weighed in the
  Balance.

God's Mercy is water; it flows to the lowest;
I will become humble earth to be embraced by the
  Merciful.

No physician gives pills and remedies to the healthy;
I will become all pain, if I must,
to be given the Remedy.

Divani Shamsi Tabrizi 1400

The Laughter of Pomegranates

If you buy a pomegranate,
buy one whose ripeness
has caused it to be cleft open
with a seed-revealing smile.

Its laughter is a blessing,
for through its wide-open mouth
it shows its heart,
like a pearl in the jewel box of Spirit.
The red anemone laughs, too,
but through its mouth you glimpse a blackness.

A laughing pomegranate
brings the whole garden to life.
Keeping the company of the holy
makes you one of them.
Whether you are stone or marble,
you will become a jewel
when you reach a human being of heart.

Plant the love of the holy ones within your spirit;
don't give your heart to anything
but the love of those whose hearts are glad.
Don't go to the neighborhood of despair:
there is hope.
Don't go in the direction of darkness:
suns exist.

The heart guides you to the neighborhood of the
    saints;

the body takes you to the prison of water and earth.
Give your heart the food of holy friends;
seek maturity from those who have matured.

Mathnawi I, 7 1 7–7 2 6

Love the Living One

To love merely for the sake of outer beauty and color
is not love but disgrace.
The peacock's plumage is its enemy.
How many kings have died for their kingdoms?
They kill the musk deer for its scent.
They skin the fox for its pelt.
They take down the great elephant for its ivory.

They may kill you for what is not really yourself.
And they think your blood will lie quiet.
Today it lies on the victim;
tomorrow it will be on the killer.
However long the shadow cast by the wall,
the shadow returns to what cast it.
This world is the mountain; each action
is like a shout that echoes back.

Love of the dead does not last,
because the dead will not return.
But love of the living
is in every moment fresher than a bud,
both to the inward and the outward eye.
Choose the love of that Living One
who is everlasting, who offers you
the wine that increases life.
Do not say, "We have no entrance to that King."
Dealings with the generous are not difficult.

Mathnawi I, 2 1 7–2 1 9; 2 2 1

The Ripening

Because of Your love I clap and dance;
drunk beyond myself, I don't know what else to do.

My raw grapes have ripened,
I can't make myself sour again.

The sweet-smelling Beloved is sugar Herself;*
She put lumps of sweetness in my mouth.

---

* In Persian the third person pronoun is ungendered. In order not
to be limited by gender, we have chosen to begin with the feminine
and switch the gender of the pronoun halfway through this *ghazal*.

Once She opened up her shop of delicacies,
She tore the roof off my shop and put me out of
    business.

People say: "You shouldn't be like that."
I wasn't like this—She made me like that.

At first She broke the vat and the vinegar spilled;
I worried that She took a loss on me.

But for that one vat, She gave a hundred vats
specially for me, and made me laugh.

In Her furnace of pain and sacrifice
She baked and toasted me like bread.

I grew old like Zulaikha* from sorrow,
but a Joseph prayed for me, and I became young
    again.

---

* Zulaikha, the wife of an Egyptian ruler, attempted unsuccessfully
to seduce the prophet Joseph. Her story is a well-known trope in
Islamic literature. Eventually her unrequited love led her to com-
munion with the Divine.

Like an arrow I would fly off His hand,
but He took me in hand and made me a bow.

Now I fill heaven and earth with thankfulness,
for I was earth, and He turned me into heaven.

My heart traveled the path of the galaxies,
but He took me beyond the galaxies.

I saw plenty of ladders and roofs,
but He made me free from both ladder and roof.

When my fame spread throughout the world,
He hid me in the world like the soul within the body.

When He found me soft like a tongue,
He translated me into a new language.

I was a tongue connected to the heart,
and He revealed the secrets of the heart, one by one.

But when my tongue began to shed blood
like a sword, He sheathed me.

Stop, O heart! For what that tender Beloved did
can never be said in words.

Divani Shamsi Tabrizi 971

I Will Mess You Up

If you fall in love with Me, I will mess you up;
cultivate little, or I will ruin you.

If you make two hundred homes like the bees do,
I will make you as homeless as a fly.

If you intend to bewilder people,
I intend to make you drunk and dazed.

If you are Mount Qaf, I will set you in motion
  like a millstone and spin you like a wheel.

And if you are a Plato or Luqman in knowledge,*
I will turn you unlearned with a single look.

---

* Luqman is mentioned in the Qur'an 31:11 as "a man of wisdom."

You are in My hand like a dead bird,
and I am a hunter; I'll make you a bait for the birds.

If you are slumbering on a treasure like a serpent,
I will make you writhe like a wounded snake.

Whether you bring reasons or not,
I will make you the convincing proof in your
    reasoning.

Whether you utter *la haul* or you don't,*
I will make you the *la haul* of the Satan like meteors.

How long would you remain captive to this or that?
If you come out of this, I will make you That.

O Shell! When you come to our Ocean,
I will make you a pearl maker, the mother of pearls.
No swords would be able to cut your throat,
if I sacrifice you like Ishmael.

---

* *La haula wa la quwwata illa billah* (There is no power nor strength
except in God); that is, there is no striving against fate; also, an ex-
clamation uttered on any sudden or perplexing emergency to drive
away evil spirits.

You are like Abraham; have no fear of fire,
I will make a hundred rose gardens from the fire.

Hold on to Our sleeve, if your own sleeves are
    stained,
so that I make you a shirt of light shining like
    moonlight.

I am the Bird of Paradise, and if I cast a shadow over
    your head,
I'll make you the King of Kings and a Sultan.

Take care! Read less! Keep silent!
So that I may recite and make you a living Qur'an!

Divani Shamsi Tabrizi 1665

What the Beloved Will Do

Beware! Don't despair if the Beloved turns you down.
If He sends you away today,
might He not call you to Himself tomorrow?

If He shuts the door on you, wait there and don't go
    away.

After testing your patience,
He will give you the seat of honor.

And if He bars all the ways and passes over you,
later He will show you the hidden way that no one
    knows.

When a butcher slaughters a ewe with a dagger and
    chops its head off,
he doesn't abandon it but takes it with him.

When the ewe's breath is gone, he fills it with his
    own breath.
So see to what wonderful places God's breath takes
    you.

But I offer this as just an example;
surely His generosity does not kill anyone
but will save from killing.

He will grant the whole kingdom of Solomon to
    an ant.
He will give away the two worlds
to prevent frightening a single heart.

My heart wandered through the whole world
and found none like Him.
Who is like Him in this world? Who does He
    resemble?

Shhhhh! Be silent! Without speech He will cause
    everyone to taste this wine;
surely, He will cause everyone to taste this wine.

Divani Shamsi Tabrizi 765

I Was Dead but I Came to Life

I was dead, but I came to life; I was all tears, I turned
    into laughter.
The authority of Love arrived, and I became Love's
    authority.

My eyes are saturated with all I've seen, my soul is
    brave;
my spirit is like a lion, and so I was made the radiant
    Venus.

He said: "You're not out of your mind, nor fit for this
    house."
I became so crazy they wanted to put me in chains.

He said: "You're not drunk enough; go away, you're
    not one of us.
I got really drunk, full of joy.

He said: "You're neither dead nor glistening with joy."
I let myself be defenseless and was slain before His
    life-giving Face.

He said: "You're so smart, intoxicated with your own
    imagination and suspicions."
I turned into an idiot, embarrassed myself, and left
    everything.

He said: "You've become a candle, the *qibla** to this
    gathering."
There is no gathering, no candle; I'm less than
    wafting smoke.

---

* The direction in which Muslims pray, namely toward the Kaaba
in Mecca.

He said: "You're a shaykh, an authority, a celebrity, a boss."
I am not a shaykh, nor a celebrity; I'm just a servant of Your command.

He said: "You have your wings and fancy feathers; I offer you neither."
Wishing for true wings and feathers, I stripped away my own plumage.

The new Dominion told me: "Don't try so hard, don't trouble yourself;
Since by My favor and abundance I am coming to you Myself."

The ancient Love told me: "Do not separate from me!"
I said: "Of course I won't." And settled down permanently.

You are the fountain of the rising sun; I am the shade of the willow.
You struck me on the head; I became humble and melted.

My heart found radiance from the soul; it opened up
and cleaved.
My heart wove new satin, and I became aloof to this
ragged garb.

This physical form that covers my soul keeps talking
nonsense at dawn:
"I was a slave and a donkey driver; I became a
soverign and a lord."

Your paper wrapper is thankful of Your abundant
candy, saying,
"When it came to my bosom, I became one and the
same with it."

My fortress of dirt is thankful for my circling
heavens.
Because He turned His attention toward me, I can
receive light.

The revolving heaven is thankful to the King, the
sovereign, and the angels,
"By His bounty and generosity, I've become
forgiving and illumined."

God's mystic is thankful to everyone and learns from
  everyone;
within the seven heavens I have become a shining
  sun."

I was the evening star; I became a moon, turning into
  a hundred-layered sphere.
I was Joseph; from now on I'll beget many Josephs.

I belong to You, O celebrated Moon; look at Yourself
  and see me!
Because of Your welcoming smile, I've become a
  smiling rose garden.

Be silent as a game of chess, let the moves speak for
  themselves.
Didn't the face of that King of the world, Shams,
  finish the game.*

Divani Shamsi Tabrizi 1393

---

* Literally, "make a beautiful-faced winner."

4

Feminine and Divine

Heaven and Earth Do Intelligent Work

Surely there is a window from heart to heart:
they are not separate or far from each other.
Though two earthenware lamps are not joined,
their light mingles.

No lover seeks union without the beloved also seeking,
but the love of lovers makes the body
thin as a bowstring,
while the love of loved ones
makes them shapely and pleasing.

When the lightning of love for the beloved
has shot into this heart,

know that there is love in that heart.
When love for God has been doubled in your heart,
there is no doubt that God has love for you.

No sound of clapping comes forth
from only one hand.
The thirsty man is moaning, "O delicious water!"
The water is calling,
"Where is the one who will drink me?"
This thirst in our souls is the magnetism of the Water:
we are Its, and It is ours.

Divine wisdom decreed us lovers of each other;
all the particles in the world
are fated to be in love with their mates,
just as amber attracts straw.
Heaven says to Earth, "Welcome,
we are magnetized to each other."

To the intellect Heaven is masculine, Earth is
    feminine;
whatever Heaven sends down,
it is the Earth's to nurture.
If Earth grows cold, Heaven sends warmth;
when Earth gets dry, Heaven pours down rain.

Heaven is almost giddy when it enters the world
   of Time,
like a husband who goes out to find
something to bring home to his wife;
and Earth is a good wife:
it gives birth and suckles what it bears.

Heaven and Earth do intelligent work.
Why else would these two nestle like lovers
if they did not taste delight in each other?

The desire in the female for the male
is so that they might perfect each other's work,
and the world is preserved by this union.

                Mathnawi III, 4391–4415

Woman, a Ray of God

She, whose beautiful face could enslave a man,
she, whose haughtiness makes your heart tremble,
how will you cope when she falls trembling in front
   of you?

She from whose disdain your heart and soul bleed,
what will you do when she starts begging you?

God has arranged it.
How can they escape what *has been made beautiful.**
Because the Divine created her
that he might take comfort in her,†
how can Adam be separated form Eve?

Though he be a hero like Rustam or Hamza,‡
he is really the captive of his old lady.
The Prophet, to whose words the whole world
  surrendered,
used to cry to Aisha:§ "Speak to me my darling
  redhead!"

Water may extinguish a fire,
unless you put it in a cauldron,
but the cauldron allows fire to dominate the water
and turn it to steam.

---

* Qur'an 40:64, 64:3
† Qur'an 2:187
‡ Rustam was a hero of Persian epics, and Hamza was a great
warrior and a noble companion of the Prophet Muhammad.
§ A beloved wife of Muhammad.

If outwardly you dominate your wife,
inwardly you are dominated,
seeking her love.

The Prophet said, "Woman
prevails over the wise man,
while the raw and ignorant prevail over her."
Those men who lack tenderness and affection
are animals, not men.

She is not that kind of beloved most imagine;
she is a ray of God.
She is not just a created,
she is creative.

Mathnawi I, 2421–2437

Lovers Are Made Aware

You resolve a hundred times
to journey somewhere,
but He draws you somewhere else.
He turns the horse's bridle in every direction

so that the untrained horse may realize there is a rider.
A good horse has a well-paced trot
when it feels a good rider on its back.

First he fixed your heart on a hundred passionate
    desires,
then disappointed you, and finally broke your heart.
Since He broke the wings of your first intention,
how do you doubt the existence of the Wing
    Breaker?
Since His ordainment
snapped the cord of your plans,
how can you remain blind to His command?

But sometimes your resolutions and aims are fulfilled
so that through hope your heart
might form another intention,
which He may once again destroy.
For if He were to keep you completely from success,
you would despair, and then
how would the seed of expectation be sown?
If your heart did not sow that seed
and then encounter barrenness,
how would it recognize its submission to Divine will?

By their failures lovers are made aware of their Lord.
Lack of success is the guide to Paradise:
pay attention to the tradition
"Paradise is encompassed with pain."*

Mathnawi III, 4456–4467

In Mutual Embrace

The desire in the female for the male
is so that they may perfect each other's work.
God put desire in man and woman
in order that the world
should be preserved by this union.
God instills the desire of every part for the other:
from their union, creation results.

And so night and day are in mutual embrace:

they appear to be opposites, even enemies,
but the truth they serve is one,

---

* Hadith of the Prophet Muhammad.

each desiring the other like kin,
for the perfection of their work.
Both serve one purpose, for without night,
human nature would receive no income:
what then could day expend?

Mathnawi III, 4414–4420

5

The Path

Songs of Unknowingness

Come down among us, be one of us lovers,
so that we may open up to you
the gate to the garden of love.

Come reside in our house like a shadow,
for we are neighbors to the Sun.

Although like the soul we are invisible in the world;
although like the love of lovers we are without a sign,

yet every sign of ours
can be traced back to You,
for just like the soul
we are both hidden and manifest.

Whatever you think us to be,
look further up; we are above that.

You are water, but in a whirlpool and engulfed;
come down among us, since we are outpouring
    torrents.

Inasmuch as we have staked our all in pure poverty,
we know nothing except singing
these songs of unknowingness.

Divani Shamsi Tabrizi 1536

Movement

If a tree could move from place to place,
It would escape the pain of the ax.

And if the sun and moon were set in stone,
how could they spread their light?

How bitter would the great Euphrates, Tigris, and
    Oxus rivers become,
if they were stagnant as a lake.

If air is confined in a well, it turns foul:
see what loss is suffered from inertia.

But when the water of the ocean rose high in the
    clouds,
it was delivered from bitterness and became fresh and
    sweet.

But when fire failed to dance in its flash and flame,
it turned to cold ash and was annihilated.

Look at Joseph of Canaan, who left his father's side,
traveled to Egypt, and became a chosen one.

Look at Moses of Imran, who left his mother
for Madyan and became a master.

Look at Jesus, son of Mary, and how he
gives life to the dead, like water from the fountain of
   life.*

Look at the Prophet, who abandoned Mecca
but to Mecca returned with an army in peace and
   dignity.

And when he journeyed to Heaven on the Night of
   Mi'raj †
he was brought close to God: *two bow lengths or nearer*.‡

I could count all the travelers of the world,
one by one, two by two, but I won't tire you.

As I revealed just a little, you yourself must take the
   rest,
depart from your own disposition, move toward
   God's disposition.

Divani Shamsi Tabrizi 214

---

* Qur'an 22:6.
† His night journey (ascension) to Heaven.
‡ Qur'an 53:9.

Nothing Happens without You

Should everything pass away,
it couldn't happen without You.
This heart of mine bears Your imprint;
it has nowhere else to turn.

The eye of intellect is drunk with You,
the wheeling galaxy is humble before You,
the ear of ecstasy is in Your hand;
nothing happens without You.

The soul is bubbling with You,
the heart imbibes from You,
the intellect bellows in rapture;
nothing happens without You.

You, my grape wine and my intoxication,
my rose garden and my springtime,
my sleep and repose;
nothing happens without You.

You are my grandeur and glory,
you are my possessions and prosperity,
you are my purest water;
nothing happens without You.

It is all Your being, Your gentle good faith
or Your seeming cruelty.
You are everything of mine;
no matter where You are going,
nothing happens without You.

They place their hearts with You,
and You break them;
they repent, You break them again.
You do all of this Yourself;
nothing happens without You.

Were something to happen without You,
the world would be overturned.
The Garden of Eden would turn to Hell;
nothing happens without You.

If You are a head, I'll become Your feet,
and if You are a fist, I'll become a flag.
If You disappear, I'll turn to nothing;
nothing happens without You.

You've disturbed my sleep,
You've effaced my personality,
You've broken every attachment;
nothing happens without You.

Should You stop being my Beloved,
my affairs would be disastrous.
My Comforter, my dear Companion!
Nothing happens without You.

Without You, life would not be delightful
nor death joyous;
how can I rebel against Your sorrow?
Nothing happens without You.

Whatever I say, O Seal of judges,
all seeming good and evil notwithstanding,
say it Yourself, by Your Grace;
nothing happens without You.

Divani Shamsi Tabrizi 553

A Stranger in Exile

Your body is of this world
and your heart is of the next.
Sensuality is a companion to this world
and God is a Companion to the next.

Your heart is a stranger in exile
and its sorrow is a stranger, too.
They belong neither
to earth nor to heaven.

If you are a companion to the soul
and a companion to wisdom,
you have reached the Beloved
and rescued your life.

And if you are a companion to the body
and a companion to sensuality,
you are alone with these two companions
in this dusty abode,

unless that Divine Favor arrives
all of a sudden.
And how much a slave I am to
such an "all of a sudden" as that.

One instant of Divine Attraction is better
than a hundred endeavors.
Of what worth are traces
before the Traceless?

View the traces as froth
and the Traceless as the ocean.
Traces are like describing
and the Traceless like seeing.

If an iota of the Sun
became manifest,
it would sweep the galaxy
right off the celestial sphere.

Be silent! Be silent!
As in silence are
thousands of tongues
and thousands of descriptions.

Divani Shamsi Tabrizi 2089

Don't Leave This House

It is *haram*, O Muslims, to leave this house,
to give up this deep red wine
and the sound of this music.

Outside, there is hypocrisy and injustice;
I've seen it a thousand times.
It would be foolish, now, to submit to those trials.

Don't leave this house, O Mad Majnun,*
or you'll bleed with tears of separation;
don't be surprised to see blood
if you've cut your own hand.

Learn nobility from a candle;
laugh while shedding tears.
Learn discretion from the eye;
move on while remaining still.

If it is your portion,
you will learn from the masters
to ascend into the blue heaven
like an innocent soul bird.

Come on, dearest one, bear Our burden with joy
so that patience may teach you
how to rise up to the ceiling that has no walls.

---

* The legendary lover of Layla whose name means "possessed by madness."

Even the incantations of Jesus, son of Mary,
did not appease the lover's pain.
The heart's grief is not allayed
by potions and incantations.

When a bowl turns upside down,
the contents run out,
but the melancholy
will not leave this skull.

Whether you are pure or impure,
do not leave this house.
For you, a servant,
there's no worse sin on earth.

You are a Soul Lion in this Court;
your opponent on the path is the fox brain.
It's not fitting for a lion to shy from this fight.

I would cleanse my heart of learning
and make myself ignorant of my self;
the Beloved has no desire for this erudition.

Souls insane with love recognize this so-called soul
to be the husk of the true Soul;

for this Knowledge one must lose
so-called knowledge and so-called sanity.

The one who breathes without breath is the best
     diver;
the one who ignores hardship is a worthy traveler.

Let go! So that the Beloved may say:
Hush . . . Repent . . .
At last we can be close.

Divani Shamsi Tabrizi 1846

Give Your Life

It suits the generous one to give money,
but truly the generosity of the lover
is to surrender the soul.
If you give bread for God's sake,
you will be given bread in return;
if you give your life for God's sake,
you will be given life in return.

If the leaves of the plane tree drop off,
it will be given the gift of leaflessness.

If because of your generosity
nothing is left in your hands,
how could God's abundance leave you downtrodden?

When a farmer sows seed, he empties the barn,
but out in the fields it's growing.
Left in the barn, time and decay,
weevil and mice, devour it.

Mathnawi I, 2235–2236

Drowned

I found true individuality in nonindividuality,
and so I wove my self into selflessness.
Since the Divine Hu* is the lover, be quiet;
when He is pulling at your ear, be all ear.

Channel the torrent when it floods
so that it won't bring shame and ruin.
But don't fear to be completely ruined,
for under the ruins waits a royal treasure.

---

* A synonym for God; it literally means "He."

When you are drowned in God,
you only want to be more drowned.
When your spirit is tossed up and down
by the waves of that Sea, you want to say,
"What's more delightful? The waves or the depths?"
And what's more fascinating:
the Beloved's shield
or His piercing arrow?

O heart, if you recognize any difference
between joy and sorrow,
these illusions will tear you apart.
Although your desire tastes sweet,
doesn't the Beloved desire you
to be desireless?

The life of lovers is in dying:
you will not win the Beloved's heart
unless you sacrifice your own.
I am drowned in a love so deep
it swallowed my first love and my last.

Mathnawi I, 1735, 1743–1749, 1751, 1757

Whirling

Whirling* is the peace of the soul for the living ones;
only the one with the Soul of the soul knows it.

Only the one who is asleep in the rose garden
should want to wake up.

But the one who is sleeping in a prison
would be worse off awake.

Whirl where there is a wedding,
not in mourning, nor in lamentation.

The one who has not seen his own essence,
the one from whose eyes that Moon is hidden,

for such a person what use is *sema* and *daf*?†
Sema is to unite with the Beloved who took your
    heart.

Those who turn in the direction of prayer,
whirl in both this world and the next.

---

* *Sema:* ecstatic listening and whirling.

† A frame drum played with the hands.

Pay heed, when a circle of friends whirl,
circling round and round, the Kaaba is the center.

If you wish a mine of sugar, it is there;
and if you wish a fingertip of sugar, it is gratis.

Divani Shamsi Tabrizi 339

Open the Window

There's a street where the Beautiful One
is known to take a stroll.

When a certain radiance is noticed
through the latticed windows
of that neighborhood,

people whisper, *The Beloved*
must be near.

Listen: open a window to God
and breathe. Delight yourself
with what comes through that opening.

The work of love is to create
a window in the heart,

for the breast is illumined
by the beauty of the Beloved.

Gaze incessantly on that Face!
Listen, this is in your power, my friend!

Find a way to your innermost secret.
Let no other perception distract you.

You, yourself, possess the elixir,
so rub it into your skin,

and by this alchemy
your inner enemies will become friends.

And as you are made beautiful,
the Beautiful One will become your own,
the intimate of your once lonely spirit.

Mathnawi VI, 3095–3097

A Sip of Poverty

A goblet of wine is worth a thousand lives;
come on then, let's pawn our clothes!

We repented of the very self of our selves;
no way we'll leave this village.

The wine makes us all one and the same color;
the small and the great become one and the same.

The dervish became empty of himself;
now let him sip this glass brimming with poverty's
    wine.

Move on and tie the bowstring on that bow,
as we are the bows and our bowstring is the wine.

The cunning intellect got stuck;
that is what the chubby old hag deserves.

We're beyond grief. Have you seen how your soul
takes on the work, while your mind does all the
    bragging!?

Escape from sorrow, go toward the King;
leave behind the rented house; go to your Eternal
Abode!

Divani Shamsi Tabrizi 2 3 5 2

Selflessness

Whether it's sugar or poison, how sweet is
selflessness!
You grab a hat, you have no head. How sweet is
selflessness!

When you fall into its trap, and try to get out but
find no escape . . .
when you take just a sip of its wine, how sweet is
selflessness!

Face your fear and be a man; you're alive, so be in
motion.
Abandon gold for a heart of gold. How sweet is
selflessness!

You spread yourself like freezing rain. Experience the
miracle of melting.

Don't be sad about this material world. How sweet is
selflessness!

Don't complain that you're trapped, that your cup of
life is full to the brim.
Find new life even in old age. How sweet is
selflessness!

How can you stay sober in this ocean of wine!
Surrender your skepticism! How sweet is selflessness!

When those black curls of Hers appear, ambergris
seems less than worthless,
but what musk, what fragrant ambergris is this sweet
selflessness!

Come on to the rose garden, friend, join the
gathering of the drunks,
A glass in every hand! How sweet is selflessness!

See the Power truly present, witnessing each and
every soul,
far beyond even selflessness. How sweet is
selflessness!

Divani Shamsi Tabrizi 2504

One Who Runs Away

Whoever runs away from our circle
runs from hearing and seeing.

A lover swallows the bleeding heart like a lion.
Without great suffering, can one ever be lionhearted?

Suppose the heart is a parrot;
then the Sweetheart offers the sugar of suffering.
Has anyone seen a parrot running away from sugar?

One who runs away is a gnat against the wind.
One who runs away is a thief fleeing from moonlight.

When God makes someone stubborn and ignorant,
that person gives up Heaven's lofty abode and flees
    to Hell.

Anyone who truly understands dying would flee
    toward death
as toward permanent life, as toward a crown and
    royal robes.

When destiny decrees that So-and-So
will die while journeying,
then So-and-So, in fear of dying, flees on a journey.

Stop it; stop hunting what is not worth hunting,
for night's fancy and even night itself will flee the
    dawn.

Divani Shamsi Tabrizi 794

6

Ecstasy

Get Ready, the Drunkards Are Coming

Little by little the bands of drunkards are coming,
little by little the wine adorers are coming.

The heart-healing ones are on the way, skipping and
dancing.
The rosy-cheeked are coming down from the rose
gardens.

Little by little from this world of being and nonbeing
the nonbeings are being gone and the true beings are
coming.

Loads of gold, or better yet, the gold mines
    themselves
are being given to the destitute!

The weak and tired ones from the meadows of love
are returning, vital and in the best of health.

The souls of the pure of heart, like beams of light
    from the sun,
are coming down from the sublime heights to these
    lowlands.

Joyous is the Garden from which, in winter,
fresh fruits of summer are brought in for Mary.

Tenderness and Grace is their origin, and so, too,
    their destination.
From fragrant orchards, they are coming toward
    fragrant orchards.

Divani Shamsi Tabrizi 819

The Face of That Beauty

It was just a glance,
but it became a fountain that drowned my heart.

If the power of that love made me seem like a pagan,
wasn't it for the face of that Beauty?

That goblet of ruby-colored wine,
that life-bestowing water of life,

that insight of eternal karma,
wasn't it for the face of that Beauty?

The calm and peace of cheerful souls,
in the shade of those interwoven curls,

in the feasting and festivity of the Great King
wasn't it for the face of that Beauty?

We lost our colors in the light of Your hue
a million miles beyond the world of existence;

the moment our souls became such idiots,
wasn't it for the face of that Beauty?

In love, an army has risen up
under the shade of the King's canopy,

and if my heart has fallen down along the way,
wasn't it for the face of that Beauty?

Bending over in sorrow like the new moon,
running headlong, facedown like the shadow,

hearing the call from within the realm of heart,
wasn't it for the face of that Beauty?

When that Moon burned up Jupiter and
broke into pieces the idols of Azar,*

then, if the heart chose infidelity,
wasn't it for the face of that Beauty?

If eighteen thousand worlds, O Soul!
were filled with my ramblings and with

---

* Abraham's father.

that flame of my inward state, O soul!
wasn't it for the face of that Beauty?

If we could do justice to the path of Love,
and if our joy could be worthy of that Moonlight and
    Sunshine,

and if we opened our eyes afresh onto that Love,
wouldn't it be for the face of that Beauty?

And by that wine whose fragrance caused my
    drunkenness,
and all the wineglasses we smashed,

and when we became free from the disgrace of self,
wasn't it by the face of that Beauty?

The garden came alive in Union,
with a spring more beautiful than all four seasons!

And Shams of Tabriz as its very essence . . .
wasn't it for the face of that Beauty?

Divani Shamsi Tabrizi 714

Ancient Wine

Not until the troubadour of the heart
sang the most dire love lament
did my Beloved stroll in with a goblet in hand

and throw into me a drunkenness of mind.
With his thousand-year-old wine
he brought the old love back to life in us.

Drunk on this moment of mine,
wine became my religion and faith.
There's nothing I want to buy
and no one I'm indebted to.

I bartered the soul's Garden of Eden
for just a winepress
and inscribed a deed for this purchase on the goblet.

O You who are scorned by time, destroy this edifice.
What I have found now
is worth more than all existence.

Shut this mouth and open the soul's,
for all the worlds seem like tiny crumbs.

This drunken soul refuses all of those crumbs, just as
    the lover
charmed by the beauties of cheek and mole sees no
    imperfection.

Heaven's souls are drunk with Shams of Tabriz.
Look how they evaporate like drops of dew!

Divani Shamsi Tabrizi 2394

Hide My Secret

This heart of mine
tugged at my collar
and led me to the village
of that Beloved of mine.

When I drank the wine
of that humble town,
I unwound my turban
and pawned even my shoes.

As I gave up my intellect
and took hold of Her ringlets,

I got tangled in the curls She loosed—
completely, beautifully entangled.

Moment by moment the wine's taking over;
see what my state has come to
with such ancient wine.
See what's happened to my mind.

She tells me, "In this drunkenness,
hide my secret and you'll be liberated."
O Muslims! In this state of mine,
how should my secrets remain concealed?

That heartbreaking Beloved tells me,
"A lover should be nothing."
O Beloved! How pushy you are!
Don't you see where I'm headed?

Like the clouds of early spring,
how I'm both sobbing and laughing!
And from these potent wines,
how joyfully I'm drunken and sober!

You'll see Mount Qaf
flying like the Anqa because of this love

if that mountain learns about
the ruby lips of my naughty Beloved.

Like the sky I am doubled up
out of love for the Tabrizi Sun.
Strum me gently,
lest my strings be broken.

Divani Shamsi Tabrizi 1413

The Dance

O Particle, it's time to dance!
Don't you know
you are the very source
of abundance, and whatever
you are seeking,
you are its very essence?

The Sun will soon reveal its face
and invite the particles to dance.
It's good to be dancing,
your clothes flying
through the air!

O Particle! One day you will clasp
the Sun to your breast.
You will put your head
next to His.
That's the point.

And He will bring out the wine, telling you:
O Particle! Drink it down!
And once you drink it,
you will merge into the soulful Sun.

A particle, after that drinking, became a sun
in the Empire of Epiphany
through the tantalizing *You shall not see Me.**

We are unripe fruits
in the radiance of Your sunlight,
but what a dance we are throwing
as You do the ripening.

Well done. Praise ripening
and tasteful drinking
granted by the soulful Sun
that has no second.

---

* Qur'an 7:143.

O Shams, my Sun! You whom I serve!
King of Kings from Tabriz!
To whom souls surrender . . .
that surrender my heart and soul know so well.

Divani Shamsi Tabrizi 2960

Madness Runs from Me

This time I'm totally
engulfed in love.
This time I'm entirely
cut off from well-being.

I've torn myself away from my self;
I'm living on something else.
Intellect, mind, and thinking itself,
I've burned to their roots.

O people! People!
I'm not capable of civility.
Even a madman wouldn't think
the thoughts I hold in my heart.

Even a madman would weep
and flee from my madness.
I've submerged in death
and passed into nonbeing.

Today my intellect
gave up on me altogether,
a feeble attempt to intimidate me.
How simple does it think I am!

Why should I worry about its leaving?
I just frowned at it!
I'm not bewildered at all!
But I can pretend to be!

Now I am free from the bowl of stars
and the blood of the celestial globe.
I, too, have often practiced flattery,
going from beggar to beggar.

Expediently I've remained
in the prison of this world,
but why, for what crime
should I be in prison?

I'm drowned in my own blood
in the prison of the body,
and because of the restive tears from my restless eyes,
I've been dragging my bloodstained skirt across this
    earth.

Like a baby in the womb,
I am being fed by blood.
Man is born once;
how many times have I been born?

Look at me as many times as you wish,
but you won't get to know me;
since you have last seen me,
I've changed a hundred times.

Come into my eyes,
and look at me through them,
for I have chosen a home
far beyond what eyes can see.

You're happy headed and dead drunk,
but I'm a happy, headless drunk.
You're a laughing lover,
but I've been laughing without a sound.

I am that rare bird who,
not because of any snare or hunter,
flew from the orchard
and perched in the cage willingly.

Being in the cage with friends is more joyful
than being in the orchard or rose garden,
and I've found rest
in the deep well with other Josephs.

I won't lament the wound the Beloved inflicts,
I won't pretend to suffer so.
I have given up a hundred sweet souls
in exchange for this affliction.

Like the silkworm in tribulation
you go about in satin and silk,
but do you hear the complaint of the silkworm
being rotted in its own long cloak?

You too have rotted away in the grave of the body.
Go to my Seraphiel and say:
"Blow your trumpet for my sake;
I'm tired of this grave."

No. No. Close your eyes to your self
like a loyal falcon.
Don't strut, like a peacock,
in rich brocades.

Bring your head to His physician,
meaning, "Give me syrup!
In this trap of amusing pleasures
I've eaten too much poison."

If you're with the beloved Confectioner,
you will be sweetened and sweet souled,
for I know what it is to flourish, like sugarcane,
on that sweetness of the soul.

Turning your very self into sweetness
is better than getting you a hundred sweets;
except from Her lips,
never have I tasted sweetness of the soul.

Better be silent; for when you speak,
sweets slip out of your mouth,
and even without your speaking,
people may catch its scent, as I have.

The unripeness of every grape
is a bitter lament that says
"Come! O Sun of Tabriz!
Deliver us from our own rawness and apathy."

Divani Shamsi Tabrizi 1372

Today

I am so, so drunk today;
I've escaped my bonds today.

I'm that "something" that doesn't occur to the mind;
I'm that; yes, I'm that, today.

Spiritually, I went up to the Heaven of the Soul,
even though in form I'm down today.

I pulled on the intellect's ear and said: "Intellect!
Be gone! Because of you I got free today!

"Take your hands off me, O mind!
I'm crazy as Majnun today."

That beautiful Joseph handed me an orange to peel.
Bewitched by His Beauty, I cut both my hands today.

That brimful Jug of Wine made me so drunk
that I broke to pieces so many earthen vats today.

I don't know where I am,
but what a happy place I'm in today!

Fortune came to my door to flirt today,
but, drunk, I slammed the door in her face.

But when she left, I ran after her;
I haven't stopped running for a moment today.

When *We are nearer than the jugular vein**
became clear today, I could no longer adore myself.

Do not tie up those ringlets of yours, Shams of
    Tabriz!
I'm caught like a fish in this net today.

Divani Shamsi Tabrizi 1185

---

* Qur'an 50:16.

Sama'

What is *sama'*?* A message from those hidden in
   the heart.
The estranged heart will be soothed by their letter.

The branches of wisdom shall blossom from this
   breeze,
and the pores shall be cleansed by this
   rubdown.

From the cry of this spiritual rooster the dawn will
   break,
and victory will be heralded by Mars's kettledrum.

The soul's essence shot arrows of wine at the jar of
   the body;
as it heard the tambourine, it began to froth.

A strange sweetness enveloped the body
as the tongue tasted the sweetness from the singer's
   lips.

---

* A gathering or ceremony during which spiritual music, poetry,
and sometimes whirling are presented.

See now a thousand scorpions of sorrow slain,
and a thousand toasts without glasses.

The feast has arrived; inscribe a charm against the
    scorpion's spell!
Isn't there always a scorpion lurking somewhere in
    love's abode?

A Jacob jumps up from every direction
as the scent of Joseph's shirt is smelled.

As our spirit is from *I breathed into him of My spirit*,"*
it is permissible that His breath would be its drink
    and food.

As the resurrection of all the people
will take place with the blowing of the trumpet,

the dead will jump out of their slumber to the joy of
hearing the whisper of love.

The one who is not moved by that blowing
is less than a nobody.

---

* Qur'an 15:29.

The body and the heart that drink from this clear and
    clean wine
are safe from the burning sorrows of separation.

Indescribable is the face of hidden Beauty;
borrow a thousand keen eyes as a loan.

Within yourself is a moon to which the sun on high
calls, "O You whose servant I'm a servant to!"

Find the moon under your own collar as Moses of
    Imran did,
and look into your own gap and say, "Salaam!"

Warm up the *sama'* and ignore the donkeys.
You are the core and kernel of *sama'*, the prosperity of
    the times.

I'll sell my tongue and buy a thousand ears
as the sweet-spoken orator goes up to the pulpit.

Divani Shamsi Tabrizi 1734

Fire in My Mouth

You've put fire in my mouth
and a hundred seals on my tongue.

The flames inside me
would roast many universes.

If this whole world were destroyed,
I'd still have a hundred more worlds after this one.

Even now caravans loaded with sugar
are approaching from the Lands of Nonexistence.

But drunk with this Love, I can't tell
if it's a profit or a loss.

The eye of the body has been scattering pearls,
    lovingly,
everywhere, from the luminous pearl of the soul.

And I will never be homebound, for like Jesus
I am at home in the Fourth Heaven.

Thanks to the One who breathes soul into the body,
if I lose my self, I still have the Soul of souls.

And what Shams of Tabriz has given me,
ask me for that, for that is what I have.

Divani Shamsi Tabrizi 1754

Go Deep, Go Deep

Here we are in this hidden corner, drunk.
O friend! These companions merged
into a single soul, drunk,

detached from the self and the world,
with mouths closed like pistachios,
breathing lightly
with the secret You gave them.

In this seclusion we are plunged in Mercy.
Clap, clap hands! For you, beloved, are of this flock.

We fell in love with lowliness,
with poverty and humbleness.
All the lofty heights are but the dust
of the gate to this lowliness.

You saw no one but yourself,
so perplexed you were in your soul.
See how squeezed you are, O Shaykh!
Become selfless and you'll set yourself free.

Close the door of the house!
Don't leave it open for strangers
to see the face unveiled,
the ringlets that were braided.

Don't do today, Dear One,
what You did yesterday,
when You played Your trick on us,
then rushed out of the house.

Although you broke away in the flesh,
you remained with us in secrecy.
You seemed to be out of sight,
but you settled in the nest of the heart.

The wits that You stole away
turned into pure wine free from dregs.
The one whom You wounded
turned into a cure for anyone who is wounded.

O heart! You fell into the arms of that Moon.
What do you want of this utterance?
O fish! The bated hook is not your friend!
Go deep, go deep.

Divani Shamsi Tabrizi 2584

Wheat

If wheat sprouts out of my grave,
the bread you make of it will get you drunk.

The baker and the dough will go insane,
and the oven will recite intoxicating verses.

If you come to visit my grave,
my tomb will make you dance.

O brother! Don't come without a tambourine,
as the sad can't join in God's celebration.

The chin has been closed tight in the grave,
yet his mouth chews the beloved's opium and
     sugarplum.

If you tear a piece off that shroud
and fasten it round your chest,
a tavern will open up from your soul.

From every direction comes the sound of the harp
and hue and cry from the drunk;
every action will perforce give rise to another one.

God has created me from love's wine;
even if death takes me, I am the same love.

I am intoxication and my origin is the wine of love;
tell me what comes from wine but intoxication?

Toward the lofty soul of Shams of Tabriz
my soul is flying, lingering not even a single moment.

Divani Shamsi Tabrizi 683

7

Love

Expanding Friendship

Money and real estate occupy the body,
but all the heart wants is expanding friendship.

A rose garden without a friend is indeed a prison;
a prison with a friend becomes a rose garden.

If the pleasure of friendship did not exist,
neither men nor women would be here.

A thorn from a friend's garden is worth more
than a thousand cypresses and lilies.

Love sewed us securely together.
We owe nothing to the needle and thread.

If the house of the world is dark,
Love will find a way to create windows.

If the world is full of arrows and swords,
the Armorer of Love has made us coats of mail.

Love itself describes its own perfection.
Be speechless and listen.

Divani Shamsi Tabrizi 1926

My Life Is through Dying

My religion is
to live through Love:

a life created from my own
small mind and self
would be a disgrace.

The blade of Love cuts away
what covers the lover's soul;
Love's sword severs sins.

When the bodily grime is gone,
a shining moon appears:
Spirit's moon in a wide-open sky.

I've beat this drum of Love
for so long, for you whom I adore,
singing: "My life depends upon my dying."

This keeps my body and soul alive.
I dream but I do not sleep.

This seagull fears no shipwreck.
Her feet love to touch the Ocean.

Mathnawi VI, 4059–4064

The Urgency of Passion

If fortune is going to be your companion,
love must have something to do with you.

A life lived without love is no life;
it adds up to nothing.

In reality we should be ashamed
of any time that passes without love.

Whatever is comfortable for you here
will be a burden when it is time to leave.

But to you who are at this moment grieved by love,
it will be as forbearing as a father.

The poverty that you are ashamed of now
will be a glory in the world to come.

However distasteful is the bitterness of patience,
it will eventually taste delicious.

The lion of the soul, when freed from this box,
will abide in the meadows of paradise.

When dismounted from this donkey's carcass,
the king of the heart will be a princely rider.

Stretch out the arms of diligence and painstaking,
and catch the gold that pours down from heaven.

You were hidden, then made manifest;
everything hidden will one day be made clear.

Whoever does not humble himself today
will one day be debased like Pharaoh.

Whoever does not melt into water like a rose in the
    fire
will burn like a thorn.

Since Nimrod was not captivated by God,
he fell prey to a gnat.

Whoever closes his eyes to the ready cash of present
    time
will be the laughingstock of expectation.

But whomever love chooses
will be intoxicated and madly in love.

Whoever is not reduced to drunkenness
    by love
will forever suffer sobriety.

Whoever does not bear the stigma of love in this
    moment
will be lost like an unbridled camel.

Whoever doesn't teach his eyes to see
will be worthless and despised.

Enough! Words settle like dust,
and dust is all that will remain of them.

Shams of Tabriz rests in peace,
yet this heart is restless for him.

Divani Shamsi Tabrizi 974

Love Is Like a Lawsuit

I am amazed at the seeker of purity
who when it's time to be polished
complains of rough handling.

Love is like a lawsuit:
to suffer harsh treatment is the evidence;
when you have no evidence, the lawsuit is lost.

Don't grieve when the Judge demands your evidence;
kiss the snake so that you may gain the treasure.

That harshness isn't toward you, O son,
but toward the harmful qualities within you.
When someone beats a rug,
the blows are not against the rug
but against the dust in it.

A few well-sifted almonds are better
than a larger number with the bitter ones mixed in.
You can't tell the difference
by the sound they make,
rattling as you pour them out.
The difference is what's inside
and the taste.

Mathnawi III, 4008–4012, 4025–4026

The Good Root

Are you fleeing from Love
because of a single humiliation?
What do you know of Love except the name?
Love has a hundred forms of pride and disdain
and is gained by a hundred means of persuasion.

Since Love is loyal, it purchases one who is loyal:
it has no interest in a disloyal companion.
The human being resembles a tree;
your root is a covenant with God:
that root must be cherished with all one's might.

A feeble covenant is a rotten root, without grace
    or fruit.
Though the boughs and leaves of the date palm
    are green,
greenness brings no benefit if the root is corrupt.
If a branch is without green leaves, yet has a good
    root,
a hundred leaves will put forth their hands in the end.

Mathnawi V, 1163–1169

How Sour Melons Become Sweet

A master had a slave named Luqman
whom he loved *so* much,
when food came, he would give it to Luqman
    first;
only then would he eat it himself,

becoming enraptured with his leftovers.
What an infinite affinity this was.
He had no taste for any food Luqman did not touch.

One day the gift of a melon arrived,
and it was sliced for Luqman to try.
He ate it with such sweet pleasure
that after seventeen slices
the master asked to taste the last.
Its sourness blistered his mouth.

"O Soul of the World," the master said,
"How did you turn this poison into an antidote?
How did you turn cruelty into kindness?
Have you made your own life your enemy?
Couldn't you find some excuse
not to eat this bitter fruit?
Luqman said, "Through your generous hands
I have tasted so much sweetness,
I could not make a fuss over some bitter rind.
Better the dust of a thousand roads cover me.
I enjoyed the melon because it came to me from you.

By love what is bitter becomes sweet,
bits of copper turn to gold.

By love the dregs are made clear,
and pain begins to heal.
By love the dead come alive,
and a king becomes a slave.

This love, moreover, is the fruit of knowledge;
no fool will ever sit on the throne of love.
When did a lack of knowledge
ever give birth to this love?
No, ignorance only falls in love
with what is lifeless.
It thinks it sees in something lifeless
the appearance of the one it desires,
as if it heard the beloved whistle.

Ignorance cannot discern;
it mistakes a flash of lightning for the sun.
When the Prophet said "The deficient are accursed,"
he meant deficiency of mind,
for perfecting the mind is possible.
Deficiency of body attracts mercy—
It is no sin to be blind.*

---

* Qur'an 48:17.

While the self-chosen pharaonic deficiency of mind
banishes you from His presence.

Lightning is transient and faithless.
Without clearness you will not know
the transient from the permanent.
Why is lightning said to laugh?
It is laughing at whoever
sets his heart upon its light.

The lights of the sky are feeble;
they are not like that Light which is neither
of the East nor the West.
See that lightning as something that
taketh away the sight,*
and regard the eternal light as a Helper.

To ride your horse on the foam of the sea,
to read your letter by the flash of lightning
is to fail, because of desire,
to see the end result.
It is to laugh
at your own mind and intelligence.

---

* Qur'an 2:20.

Intelligence, by its nature, sees the end;
it is your animal side that cannot see the end.
Intelligence overwhelmed by the flesh
becomes flesh; Jupiter checkmated by Saturn
turns inauspicious.

Yet turn your gaze toward this bad luck
and see the One who brought it to you.
Whoever witnesses this ebb and flow
penetrates from bad luck to good.
God continually turns you
from one state of feeling to another,
revealing truth by means of dualities . . .
so that you may have two wings;
for the bird with one wing is unable to fly.

One needs the spirit of an Abraham
to intuit Paradise and its mansions in the fire.
Go, step-by-step, beyond the moon and sun.
Don't remain a door knocker on a door.
This bodily world is deceptive,
except for one who has transcended desires.

Mathnawi II, 1510–1560

Rare Soul Wine

If all the world is full of thorns,
the lover's heart will be a bed of roses.

Even if the sphere of stars stops turning,
the world of lovers keeps going on.

Everybody gets sad sometime,
but the lover's soul keeps a tender smile.

Give the lover an unlit candle,
and he'll awaken it with his own light.

Although alone, a lover is never lonely,
forever with the hidden Beloved.

The lovers' wine spills out of their chests;
they give their love in secret ways.

Love will not be satisfied with a hundred promises,
for those who steal your heart away have so many
 tricks.

If you see a lover feigning sick,
expect the beloved to soon be at the bedside.

Ride on love and don't worry about the road!
Because the steed of love has the smoothest ride.

It will take you home in a single thrust,
even though the road is rough.

You won't find lovers munching in the pasture.
Lovers sip a rare soul wine.

From Shams of Tabriz you will find
a heart very drunk and truly sober.

Divani Shamsi Tabrizi 662

The Town of Love

I traveled around from town to town,
But I saw nothing like the Town of Love.

From the beginning, I did not know the value of that
place
and in ignorance had to suffer the misery of exile.

I abandoned such a land of honey as that
to graze on all kinds of grass like an animal.

Why, like the people of Moses, did I
prefer garlic and onions to manna and quails!?*

Apart from love, every sound that I heard in the
    world
sounded like a banging drum.

By the sound of that drum, I fell from the Court of
    Heaven
down to this perishable world.

I was a solitary self among so many others,
flitting around like a wingless, footless heart.

From that wine, which bestows grace and laughter,
I was drinking, as a flower does, with no lips or
    throat.

---

* Referring to the *ayah* (a verse of the Qur'an), "And remember ye
said: 'O Moses! We cannot endure one kind of food [always]; so be-
seech thy Lord to produce for us of what the earth grows,—its pot-
herbs, and cucumbers, its garlic, lentils, and onions'" (Qur'an 2:61).

Then there came a call from Love, "O soul!
Leave this abode of drudgery I created for you."

Often I would say, "I don't like it down there,"
and would bitterly moan and tear my clothes.

Just as I am scared of departing now,
I was also reluctant to leave then.

He said, "O soul! Get going! Wherever you are,
I am as near to you as your jugular vein."*

He enchanted me with so many sweet words,
and I took them to heart.

His enchantment causes the whole world to bounce
   high.
Who am I? I'm invisible even to myself.

First He led me from the Way
and then brought me back to the Way,

---

* Referring to the *ayah* "We are nearer to him than his jugular vein"
(Qur'an 50:16).

but had I not strayed from the Way,
how would I have known the snare of His love?

I would tell you how to get here, but
at this point, my pen is broken.

Divani Shamsi Tabrizi 1509

Not with My Own Breath

Though I can't express what this flirtation is,
I have only Your love within my heart.

If ever I smell a flower without Your love,
set me ablaze like thorns.

If ever I am quiet like a fish,
make me restless like waves upon the sea.

You who have put a seal upon my lips,
pull my bridle in Your direction!

What's Your purpose? How should I know?!
All I know is that I am on this caravan.

I contemplate Your sorrow, like a camel its fodder;
like a tipsy camel I foam and froth.

However much I conceal, not speaking a word,
in the presence of Love, it all spills out.

Like a seed, I am buried in the earth,
waiting for spring to call

so that I may exhale with joy,
but not with my own breath;
so that I may scratch my head,
no longer my own head.

Divani Shamsi Tabrizi 1562

What Am I?

With all of these many-faced I's and we's,
what sort of "I" am I?
Listen, take your hand off my mouth
and let me rave.

I'm already lost.
Don't lay shattered glass in my path;
I'll crush whatever's in my way.

With every breath my heart
is stupefied by the vision of You.
If You're happy, I'll be happy;
if You're sad, I'll be sad, too.

If You're bitter, I'll be embittered;
if You're tender, I'll be tender as well.
My only joy is to be with You,
close to Your sweet lips and delicate chin, Beloved.

Everything depends on You. Who am I?
Just a mirror in Your hand.
Whatever You reveal, that's what I am;
I'm just a polished mirror.

If You're a graceful cypress,
I'm Your shadow;
and when you're a flower,
like your shadow, I'll pitch my tent nearby.

If I pluck a flower without You,
it becomes a thorn in my hand,
and if I'm a thorn,
with You I become roses and jasmine.

Moment by moment my heart
sheds tears of blood; then with a sudden breath
I smash my glass
at the door of the wine server.

If ever I try to reach for some idol,
I get my face scratched, my shirt torn.

From somewhere beyond myself
grace radiates into my heart.
Somewhere a Candle illumines this whole world.
Who am I? Just the candlestick holder.

Divani Shamsi Tabrizi 1397

You, You, You

Beloved, You are my cave.
You are the fire of love that consumes me.
The beloved is You; the cave is You.

The Prophet Noah is You; spirit is You.
The conqueror and the conquered.
This chest torn into pieces is You.
The one knocking at the door of the secret is me.

You are the light; You are the celebration.
The protection of those who are protected,
the bird over Mount Sinai is You.
The exhausted prey in its beak is me.

The drop is You; the ocean is You.
The gift and the wrath are You.
The sugar is You; the poison is You.
Grant me no more pain.

The signs of the Sun are You.
The house of Mercury is You.
The path of hope is You.
Grant me the Way.

The day is You; the fasting is You.
The result of my begging is You.
Water is You; the ewer is You.
Give me the water this time.

The grain is You; the trap is You.
The wine bottle is You; the cup is You.
The cooked is You; the raw is You.
Don't leave me uncooked.

If this body becomes more refined,
the pathways inside my heart pump more freely.
Become my path completely, so there will be
so much less for me to say.

Divani Shamsi Tabrizi 37
Translated by RAHA AZAR
AND KABIR HELMINSKI

The Battle of Love

This battle of Love is getting hotter.
The source of its heat is beyond time and space:
from the sparks of its fire the smoke of seven Hells is
rising.

But Hell is extinguished by Love's burning.
Hell says to the sincere lover, "Go quickly,
or my fire will be destroyed by your flames."

Watch how this breath of Love dissolves
unfaithfulness, the brimstone of Hell!
Offer your brimstone to this passionate Love,

and neither these Hells
nor what sparks them
will assail you.

Paradise, too, says to the lover,
"Pass over me like the breeze,
or all I possess will become unsalable;

"for you are the original owner
and I'm just the advertisement:
I am the idol, while you are the reality."

Both Hell and Paradise tremble
before the man or woman of faith:
neither feels safe in the presence of the truly faithful.

Mathnawi VI, 4606–4614

Love Ends All Arguments

The greatness of the Kaaba as a place of gathering
is measured by the expanse of desert
and the brigands along the way.
Every belief or doctrine that does not lift you up
is like a brigand or a treacherous mountain pass.
When doctrines become bitter enemies,
the imitator is perplexed at the crossroads.
He sees that both ways go somewhere,
and every group is pleased by its own path.
And even if it cannot reply to criticisms of its way,
the group will cling to it until the resurrection, saying,
"Our experts know the answer even if we don't."

But only Love dissolves doubt and banishes
      temptation.
Become a lover, follow that crane from river to river.
How will you have that water
with someone who drains your water away?
How will you perceive the Truth
with someone who consumes your apprehension?
With Love you will discover an intelligence
beyond these intelligible things.
By one kind of intelligence you earn a living;

by this other you ascend the carpeted tiers of heaven.
When you gamble your intelligence away in Love,
He multiplies it by ten, or by seven hundred.

Remember those women of Egypt
who lost their minds
in the presence of the handsome Joseph?
The cupbearer of Life took their minds away in a
    single moment,
but they drank from the cup of wisdom
for the rest of their lives.
You could wish to be as much in love as those
    women,
but there is another Beauty that would blow Joseph
    away.

Dear soul, Love alone cuts arguments short,
for it alone comes to the rescue
when you cry for help against disputes.
Eloquence is dumbfounded by Love:
it dares not wrangle,
for the lover fears that if he answers back,
the pearl of inner experience
might fall out of his mouth.
His lips are sealed.

A companion of the Prophet said:
"Whenever the Messenger recited revelation to us,
he would demand complete attentiveness."
It's as if a bird had perched on your head,
and your soul wants it to stay.
You don't cough, you hardly breathe,
and if someone else starts talking,
you put your finger to your lips: *shhhh*.
Astonishment is the bird that silences you.
It puts a lid on your kettle
so that you boil.

Mathnawi V, 3224–3250

Like This . . .

If anyone asks you what the virgins of Paradise are like,
show your face, as if to say, "Like this . . ."

If anyone asks you about the rising moon,
go up to the roof, as if to say, "Like this . . ."

If anyone boasts about the fragrance of musk,
just let down your hair and say, "Like this . . ."

And if they say, "How do clouds part to reveal the
    full moon?"
undo the ties of your robe one by one and say,
    "Like this . . ."

If anyone asks you how Jesus brought the dead to life,
kiss us publicly on the lips, as if to say, "Like this . . ."

And if he says, "Tell us what it's like to lose your life
    for love,"
present my soul to him, as if to say, "Like this . . ."

Whoever out of compassion asks about my stature,
reveal your bent eyebrow, meaning "Like this . . ."

Some say the soul leaves the body,
then returns to it again;
show those in denial how you come back home,
    meaning "Like this . . ."

From every direction that you hear the lovers' lament,
it's all our story, by God, meaning "Like this . . ."

This bruised chest is a refuge for any angel,
look up tenderly toward the sky, meaning
    "Like this . . ."

The secret of union with the Friend, I've shared only
    with the breeze,
now it's a secret only the pure breeze can tell, like
    this . . .

And if they cynically assert, "How does anyone reach
    the Truth?!"
place a candle of purity in the palm of each one's
    hand, meaning "Like this . . ."

I said, "How does the scent of Joseph travel from
    town to town?"
The scent of Truth wafted up from the world of Hu
    "like this . . ."

I said, "How could the scent of Joseph give sight back
    to my eyes?"
Your breeze gave light to my eyes like this . . .

The Sun still shines generously from Tabriz.
It rises up in loyalty and tenderness like this . . .

Divani Shamsi Tabrizi 1826

Cosmic Smoke

Lovers please God.
In the end they are the most blessed!

Give them a feast of Your Beauty!
Let their souls smolder like aloeswood in Your fire!

Dip Your Hand in our blood, Beloved.
Take our bloodstained souls in Your hands!

If anyone prays: "Let her escape this love,"
Heaven just laughs!

See how thin the moon is
for a while on the way of love;
that lack becomes its beauty!

Others ask for a respite from death;
the lovers say: "No, let it come now."

Heaven is filled with the incense of lovers.
O Creator of this cosmic smoke, Well done!

Divani Shamsi Tabrizi 826

You Are Joy and We Are Laughter

O my God, our intoxicated eyes have blurred our
    vision.
Our burdens have been made heavy, forgive us.

You are hidden, and yet from East to West
You have filled the world with Your radiance.
Your Light is more magnificent than sunrise or
    sunset,
and You are the inmost ground of consciousness
revealing the secrets we hold.

You are an explosive force
causing our dammed-up rivers to burst forth.
You whose essence is hidden
while Your gifts are manifest,
You are like water and we are like millstones.
You are like wind and we are like dust.

The wind is hidden while the dust is plainly seen.
You are the invisible spring,
and we are Your lush garden.
You are the Spirit of life and we are like hand and foot.
Spirit causes the hand to close and open.

You are intelligence; we are Your voice.
Your intelligence causes this tongue to speak.
You are joy and we are laughter,
for we are the result of the blessing of Your joy.

All of our movement is really
a continual profession of faith,
bearing witness to Your eternal power,
just as the powerful turning of the millstone
professes faith in the river's existence.

Dust settles upon my head and upon my metaphors,
for You are beyond anything we can ever think or say.
And yet, this servant cannot stop trying
to express Your Beauty;
in every moment,
let my soul be Your carpet.

Mathnawi V, 3307–3319
Translated with CAMILLE HELMINSKI

The Last Weight

Love is honey for the grown-up
and milk for children:
for every boat it is the last weight
that causes that boat to sink.

Mathnawi VI, 3998

Born from Love

On the way of Love you must be very alive.
The lifeless have nothing to give.
So, who is alive?
The one who is born from Love.

The vehemence of the roaring lion,
the sharpness of the piercing sword,
the machismo of all males,
come to bluntness before Love.

There are waylayers in the way, too;
beware these unmanly companions.
With fancy shoes
this way may not be fared.

Listen: Battle drums are beating;
the troops of Love are marching.
Where is the heroic soul
who will give the sign?

Thunder will rumble from the heart.
From out of the body the soul will flash
just as from a tumbling cloud
lightning strikes.

Never will sorrow
take hold of such a heart.
All the world's sorrows
only expand its rapture.

The whole ocean shrinks
before the storm of early spring.
The world is sweet because of lovers,
though some spin a different story.

This lion hunts no deer.
His deer is the presence of "Ya Hu,"
while unbelieving critics
chew thorns in their pasture.

In Love, search for us!
In us, search for This!
At times we adore;
at other times *we* feel adored.

So, like an oyster shell,
that Presence opens its mouth
to swallow like a drop
this whole ocean called "me and us."

Divani Shamsi Tabrizi 843

Index of First Lines